About the author

Bishop Dr. David Oronsaye is a prophet to the Nations, a seasoned preacher with a mandate to stir up the body of Christ for the end time move of God. He functions powerfully in the prophetic, with signs and wonders following.

A true evangelist driven with a strong passion for the lost, he is also an author of several inspirational books.

He is the co-founder and general overseer of the All Nations Christian Centre international headquarters in London, England.

He is married to Rev. Judith Oronsaye and they are blessed with four daughters.

All Nations Christian Centre
15 York Hill, West Norwood,
London, SE27 0BU
E-mail: drdavid.ancc@gmail.com
Tel: +44 (0)20 8670 0300

Website: www.anccministries.org

Dedication

I dedicate this book to my
Inspirer,
Leader
and Teacher:
the Holy Spirit.

Do not worry about tomorrow,
for tomorrow will
worry about itself.
Each day has enough
trouble of its own.

(Matthew 6:34).

The Power of Value

Bishop Dr. David Oronsaye

Published in the United Kingdom by
Filament Publishing Ltd
16 Croydon Road, Waddon, Croydon,
Surrey, CR0 4PA, United Kingdom
+44(0)20 8688 2598
www.filamentpublishing.com

© 2015 Bishop Dr. David Oronsaye

ISBN 978-1-910819-34-0

Printed by IngramSpark

The right of Bishop Dr. David Oronsaye to be identified as the author of this work has been asserted by him in accordance with the Designs and Copyright Act 1988.

This book is subject to international copyright and may not be copied in any way without the prior written permission of the publishers.

All Scripture quotations are from the New International Version of the Bible, except otherwise stated.

TABLE OF CONTENTS

Acknowledgements		8
Introduction		9
Chapter One	What is Value?	11
Chapter Two	Advantage of Value in Church and Organisation	19
Chapter Three	Improving your Organisation's Value	37
Chapter Four	Promoting Church Values	49
Chapter Five	Power of Value	62
Chapter Six	Value and Fear of God	70
Chapter Seven	Jesus' Primary Objectives	83
Chapter Eight	God's Concept of Value	103
Chapter Nine	Value and Accountability	111
Chapter Ten	Value Prayer Points	120

Acknowledgements

I would like to thank the following people for their support, effort and encouragement:

Firstly, I would like to thank God for His anointing upon my life as Prophet to the nations.

I thank God for His Holy Spirit that inspired me to write this book.

I thank God for my wife Rev. Judith Oransaye as she supports me in ministry and my four daughters.

I also thank my editors, and I thank God for all the people that have been blessed by my ministry.

Introduction

Value initiates your celebration and you are celebrated because you are worth it. You are significant, costly, have weight of value and are highly rated. *The Power of Value* gives a clear understanding of assessment in a believer's life and how church value is promoted. Prayer points are also included to be used according to individual needs.

It is open revelation that solution is better than problem. It is good for believers to develop the mentality of solution. This means seeking for solution whenever problems appear because as a Christian, you are the solution. Some people glory in problem than solution, but it should be the other way round. Value initiates protection which means we protect what we value.

David fought against Goliath because he valued the nation of the Israelites and also because he valued the integrity of God and his word; hence David fought and killed Goliath. He embraced his nation and God stood with him and destroyed Goliath, through David's available instrument (1Samuel 17). The Bible scriptures used in this book are New International Version (NIV).

You can only be celebrated
if you are worth it.
If you have no weight,
you cannot be celebrated,
if you are not doing
something worth celebrating.

Chapter One
WHAT IS VALUE?

Your values are the things that you believe are important, and it shows in the way you live and work. They (should) determine your priorities and, deep down, they are probably the measures you use to tell if your life is turning out the way you want it to. When the things that you do and the way you behave match your values, life is usually good – you're satisfied and content. But when these don't align with your values, that's when things feel... wrong. This can be a real source of unhappiness.

Therefore I tell you, do not worry about your life, what you will eat or drink; or about your body, what you will wear. Is not life more than food and the body more than clothes? Look at the birds of the air; they do not sow or reap or store away in barns, and yet your heavenly Father feeds them. Are you not much more valuable than they? Can any one of you by worrying add a single hour to your life?

And why do you worry about clothes? See how the flowers of the field grow. They do not labour or spin. Yet I tell you that not even Solomon in all his splendour was dressed like one of these. If that is how God clothes the grass of the field, which is here today and tomorrow is thrown into the fire, will he not much more clothe you—you of little faith? So do not worry, saying, 'What shall we eat?' or 'What shall we drink?' or 'What shall we wear?' For the pagans run after all these things, and your heavenly Father knows that you need them. But seek first his kingdom and his righteousness, and all these things will be given to you as well. Therefore do not worry about tomorrow, for tomorrow will worry about itself. Each day has enough trouble of its own (Matthew 6:25-34).

Value initiates your celebration and you are celebrated because of worth. You are significant, costly, weight of value and highly rated.

Creating Value and Celebration

No one can celebrate a mad man, person of confusion, disobedient person and a servant who destroys. Celebrating a mad man or woman with a gift is additional dishonour. This has given the power of attorney order for your arrest at approximate cause of this madness and to be released, you must withdraw the celebration and gift. A fool has neither value, nor sense of value, therefore no one can celebrate a foolish person.

Celebrating a foolish person is madness; no man of understanding can vote for a fool; it is the highest form of dishonour and multiple disgraces. No one can also celebrate a lazy person; a lazy person is a problem to themselves and to their generation. Where the laws of profit and loss account exist, a lazy person has no future; he/she is not a profit account but a loss account. Foolishness and laziness can be created through ignorance whether deliberate or not deliberate.

My people are destroyed for lack of knowledge: because thou hast rejected knowledge, I will also reject thee, that thou shalt be no priest to me: seeing thou hast forgotten the law of thy God, I will also forget thy children (Hosea 4:6).

A lazy person will end his/her life begging. Laziness initiates liability instead of being an asset. What value does a lazy person create? None, because they have not created any value, therefore they cannot be celebrated. Celebrating a liability is like celebrating confusion as well as creating confusion.

The slothful man saith, there is a lion in the way; a lion is in the streets. As the door turneth upon his hinges, so doth the slothful upon his bed. The slothful hideth his hand in his bosom; it grieveth him to bring it again to his mouth. The sluggard is wiser in his own conceit than seven men that can render a reason (Proverbs 26:13-16).

The beginning of the words of his mouth is foolishness: and the end of his talk is mischievous madness (Ecclesiastes 10:13).

Celebration and Qualification

To be celebrated requires provable evidence that qualifies for celebration. Your provable evidence reveals your created value, based on your application and manifestation in your given assignment, which will initiate your celebration.

Created Value, Evidence and Celebration

Making an impact and imparting your generation, effecting good changes, making a difference and being a difference, creates your value and initiates your celebration. You can only be celebrated if you are worth it. If you have no weight, you cannot be celebrated, if you are not doing something worth celebrating.

Create Value and Celebrate with your Natural and Supernatural Gift

Your natural ability and supernatural gifts can be used to create and have positive impact on others. That way, you will be delivering services to your generation with positive attitude, diligence and purity of discipline. This will create your value, which will initiate your reward. Ephesians 4:7-16 tells us God has a reward system if you are profitable in his Kingdom. He will reward you according to your impact (Hebrews 11:6).

You will be celebrated and rewarded when you create value through the effective use of your natural ability and supernatural gift. The value you create and gifts put to use in creating an impact in your generation, initiate your celebration and programmed announcement. It is your project which is making a difference that announces and initiates both your reward and celebration.

If you want to be celebrated, do something that is evidence based with products that will add value to others. People will look for you because your product will announce you. You cannot fold your hands and expect people to celebrate you.

There are different kinds of gifts, but the same Spirit distributes them. There are different kinds of service, but the same Lord. There are different kinds of working, but in all of them and in everyone it is the same God at work. Now to each one the manifestation of the Spirit is given for the common good.

To one there is given through the Spirit a message of wisdom, to another a message of knowledge by means of the same Spirit, to another faith by the same Spirit, to another gifts of healing by that one Spirit, to another miraculous powers, to another prophecy, to another distinguishing between spirits, to another speaking in different kinds of tongues, and to still another the interpretation of tongues. All these are the work of one and the same Spirit, and he distributes them to each one, just as he determines. Just as a body, though one has many parts, but all its many parts form one body, so it is with Christ. For we were all baptized by one Spirit so as to form one body—whether Jews or Gentiles, slave or free— and we were all given the one Spirit to drink. Even so the body is not made up of one part but of many.

Now if the foot should say, "Because I am not a hand, I do not belong to the body," it would not for that reason stop being part of the body. And if the ear should say, "Because I am not an eye, I do not belong to the body," it would not for that reason stop being part of the body. If the whole body were an eye, where would the sense of hearing be? If the whole body were an ear, where would the sense of smell be? But in fact God has placed the parts in the body, every one of them, just as he wanted them to be. If they were all one part, where would the body be? As it is, there are many parts, but one body. The eye cannot say to the hand, "I don't need you!" And the head cannot say to the feet, "I don't need you!" On the contrary, those parts of the body that seem to be weaker are indispensable, and the parts that we think are less honourable we treat with special honor. And the parts that are not presentable are treated with special modesty, while our presentable parts need no special treatment.

But God has put the body together, giving greater honor to the parts that lacked it, so that there should be no division in the body, but that its parts should have equal concern for each other. If one part suffers, every part suffers with it; if one part is honored, every part rejoices with it. Now you are the body of Christ, and each one of you is a part of it. And God has placed in the church first of all apostles, second prophets, third teachers, then miracles, then gifts of healing, of helping, of guidance, and of different kinds of tongues. Are all apostles? Are all prophets? Are all teachers? Do all work miracles? Do all have gifts of healing? Do all speak in tongues? Do all interpret? Now eagerly desire the greater gifts (1 Corinthians 12:4-31).

Again, it will be like a man going on a journey, who called his servants and entrusted his wealth to them. To one he gave five bags of gold, to another two bags, and to another one bag, each according to his ability. Then he went on his journey. The man who had received five bags of gold went at once and put his money to work and gained five bags more. So also, the one with two bags of gold gained two more. But the man who had received one bag went off, dug a hole in the ground and hid his master's money. After a long time the master of those servants returned and settled accounts with them.

The man who had received five bags of gold brought the other five. 'Master,' he said, 'you entrusted me with five bags of gold. See, I have gained five more.' 'His master replied, 'Well done, good and faithful servant! You have been faithful with a few things; I will put you in charge of many things. Come and share your master's happiness!' "*The man with two bags of gold also came. 'Master,' he said, 'you entrusted me with two bags of gold; see, I have gained two more.' 'His master replied, 'Well done, good and faithful servant! You have been faithful with a few things; I will put you in charge of many things. Come and share your master's happiness!'* "*Then the man who had received one bag of gold came. 'Master,' he said, 'I knew that you are a hard man, harvesting where you have not sown and gathering where you have not scattered seed. So I was afraid and went out and hid your gold in the ground. See, here is what belongs to you.'* "*His master replied, 'you wicked, lazy servant! So you knew that I harvest where I have not sown and gather where I have not scattered seed? Well then, you should have put my money on deposit with the bankers, so that when I returned I would have received it back with interest. 'So take the bag of gold from him and give it to the one who has ten bags. For whoever has will be given more and they will have abundance. Whoever does not have, even what they have will be taken from them. And throw that worthless servant outside, into the darkness, where there will be weeping and gnashing of teeth'* (Matthew 25:14:30).

∼

Chapter Two
THE ADVANTAGE OF VALUES IN CHURCH & ORGANISATIONS

Values initiate the following:

1. **Protection:**

What we value, we protect, fight and defend. No one can fight for useless things, because useless things have no value and to protect something which is of no value, which is seen as foolishness, is a disgrace and dishonour. David fought against Goliath because he valued the nation, Israel, the integrity of God and his word; hence David fought and killed Goliath. He embraced his nation and God stood with him and destroyed Goliath (1 Samuel 17).

2. **Maintain:**

You take care of what you value: you would not allow anyone to throw dirt on it nor give them a chance to downgrade it. You maintain and value the image of your church as an organisation and people involved with the organisation. What you do not maintain, you devaluate and it will become obsolete. That is why every organisation has set rules, protocols, policies and procedures in order to enforce values which need to be maintained. People do not value anything that cost them nothing and what they had not paid a great price for or suffered for. Anyone who paid a great price must ensure and enforce the organisation's values.

3. Respect:

Anything we value, we respect. Whatever we do not respect has lost its value and has no level of importance to us, and therefore it has no value to us. Respect initiates attraction which is the beauty of value. What you value and respect gives others a sense of positive direction and they would act as you act. When people see you as a disorganised person, they will join your club and be disorganised around you. When you are seen as an organised person, they will do the same around you.

4. Honour:

Value initiates honour. What you value will attract honour and whatever you do not value will attract dishonour. For example, if a church and its leaders are not honoured by its own people, it will create evil within the atmosphere and when the church receives new members, they will also become influenced by that evil anointing in the church. No one can receive from anything they dishonour. Whatever you dishonour will be far-reaching for you, and whatever you honour and value initiates your blessings. The anointing of God does not work for the people who do not value and honour their leaders. A lot of believers do not receive their miracles and break through because they have neglected the principles of honour based on value.

5. Publication:

Value initiates good publication and positive advertisement. What you value, you download beauty upon it. This is done through good publication and excellent advertisement.

6. Sacrifice:
Value enforces sacrifice and hard work. When value is placed on something, one will be ready to pay high price and sacrifice for it. It also takes risk in order to retain value.

7. Defence:
Defence is the highest form of protection of value. This involves a high level of security. You should defend what you value.

8. Spending Power:
What you value empowers and enforces your spending power. You will spend money on something you value because to you, it is worth it. Paying your tithes, vows and other financial contributions in order to retain objectives and visions of the organisation. This should be done with joy, excitement, and absence of evil comments and complaints.

9. Activating Attention and Responsiveness:
Value arrests attention and responsiveness. This showcases the power of value. Value creates focus and eliminates distraction and divided attention.

10. Value initiates commitment and Dedication:
Where there is an absence of value, there would also be absence of commitment and dedication. People neglect their responsibilities and assignments because of neglected values.

11. Value initiates good and positive communication:
No one will talk negative about what they value. Value helps to eliminate negative conversation. We speak positively about the things we value especially those people who recognise the power of value.

Paul said: *I want to know Christ—yes, to know the power of his resurrection and participation in his sufferings, becoming like him in his death* (Philippians 3:10).

Who shall separate us from the love of Christ? Shall trouble or hardship or persecution or famine or nakedness or danger or sword? As it is written: "For your sake we face death all day long; we are considered as sheep to be slaughtered.

No, in all these things we are more than conquerors through him who loved us. For I am convinced that neither death nor life, neither angels nor demons, neither the present nor the future, nor any powers, neither height nor depth, nor anything else in all creation, will be able to separate us from the love of God that is in Christ Jesus our Lord (Romans 8: 35- 39).

King Nebuchadnezzar made an image of gold, sixty cubits high and six cubits wide, and set it up on the plain of Dura in the province of Babylon.

He then summoned the satraps, prefects, governors, advisers, treasurers, judges, magistrates and all the other provincial officials to come to the dedication of the image he had set up. So the satraps, prefects, governors, advisers, treasurers, judges, magistrates and all the other provincial officials assembled for the dedication of the image that King Nebuchadnezzar had set up, and they stood before it.

Then the herald loudly proclaimed, "Nations and peoples of every language, this is what you are commanded to do: As soon as you hear the sound of the horn, flute, zither, lyre, harp, pipe and all kinds of music, you must fall down and worship the image of gold that King Nebuchadnezzar has set up. Whoever does not fall down and worship will immediately be thrown into a blazing furnace."

Therefore, as soon as they heard the sound of the horn, flute, zither, lyre, harp and all kinds of music, all the nations and peoples of every language fell down and worshipped the image of gold that King Nebuchadnezzar had set up.

At this time some astrologers came forward and denounced the Jews. They said to King Nebuchadnezzar, "May the king live forever! Your Majesty has issued a decree that everyone who hears the sound of the horn, flute, zither, lyre, harp, pipe and all kinds of music must fall down and worship the image of gold, and that whoever does not fall down and worship will be thrown into a blazing furnace But, there are some Jews whom you have set over the affairs of the province of Babylon—Shadrach, Meshach and Abednego—who pay no attention to you, your Majesty.

They neither serve your gods nor worship the image of gold you have set up." Furious with rage, Nebuchadnezzar summoned Shadrach, Meshach and Abednego. So these men were brought before the king, and Nebuchadnezzar said to them, "Is it true, Shadrach, Meshach and Abednego, that you do not serve my gods or worship the image of gold I have set up? Now when you hear the sound of the horn, flute, zither, lyre, harp, pipe and all kinds of music, if you are ready to fall down and worship the image I made, very good. But if you do not worship it, you will be thrown immediately into a blazing furnace. Then what god will be able to rescue you from my hand?" Shadrach, Meshach and Abednego replied to him, "King Nebuchadnezzar, we do not need to defend ourselves before you in this matter. If we are thrown into the blazing furnace, the God we serve is able to deliver us from it, and he will deliver us from Your Majesty's hand. But even if he does not, we want you to know, your Majesty that we will not serve your gods or worship the image of gold you have set up."

Then Nebuchadnezzar was furious with Shadrach, Meshach and Abednego, and his attitude toward them changed. He ordered the furnace heated seven times hotter than usual and commanded some of the strongest soldiers in his army to tie up Shadrach, Meshach and Abednego and throw them into the blazing furnace. So these men, wearing their robes, trousers, turbans and other clothes, were bound and thrown into the blazing furnace.

The king's command was so urgent and the furnace so hot that the flames of the fire killed the soldiers who took up Shadrach,

Meshach and Abednego, and these three men, firmly tied, fell into the blazing furnace. Then King Nebuchadnezzar leaped to his feet in amazement and asked his advisers "Weren't there three men that we tied up and threw into the fire?" They replied, "Certainly, Your Majesty." He said, "Look! I see four men walking around in the fire, unbound and unharmed, and the fourth looks like a son of the gods." Nebuchadnezzar then approached the opening of the blazing furnace and shouted, "Shadrach, Meshach and Abednego, servants of the Most High God, come out! Come here!" So Shadrach, Meshach and Abednego came out of the fire, and the satraps, prefects, governors and royal advisers crowded around them.

They saw that the fire had not harmed their bodies, nor was a hair of their heads singed; their robes were not scorched, and there was no smell of fire on them. Then Nebuchadnezzar said, "Praise be to the God of Shadrach, Meshach and Abednego, who has sent his angel and rescued his servants! They trusted in him and defied the king's command and were willing to give up their lives rather than serve or worship any god except their own God. Therefore I decree that the people of any nation or language who say anything against the God of Shadrach, Meshach and Abednego be cut into pieces and their houses be turned into piles of rubble, for no other god can save in this way." Then the king promoted Shadrach, Meshach and Abednego in the province of Babylon (Daniel 3:1-30).

Adam made love to his wife Eve and she became pregnant and gave birth to Cain. She said, "With the help of the Lord I have brought forth a man." Later she gave birth to his brother Abel.

Now Abel kept flocks, and Cain worked the soil. In the course of time Cain brought some of the fruits of the soil as an offering to the Lord. And Abel also brought an offering—fat portions from some of the firstborn of his flock. The Lord looked with favour on Abel and his offering, but on Cain and his offering he did not look with favour. So Cain was very angry, and his face was downcast. Then the Lord said to Cain, "Why are you angry? Why is your face downcast? If you do what is right, will you not be accepted? But if you do not do what is right, sin is crouching at your door; it desires to have you, but you must rule over it." Now Cain said to his brother Abel, "Let's go out to the field."

While they were in the field, Cain attacked his brother Abel and killed him. Then the Lord said to Cain, "Where is your brother Abel?" "I don't know," he replied. "Am I my brother's keeper?" The Lord said, "What have you done? Listen! Your brother's blood cries out to me from the ground. Now you are under a curse and driven from the ground, which opened its mouth to receive your brother's blood from your hand. When you work the ground, it will no longer yield its crops for you. You will be a restless wanderer on the earth." Cain said to the Lord, "My punishment is more than I can bear. Today you are driving me from the land, and I will be hidden from your presence; I will be a restless wanderer on the earth, and whoever finds me will kill me." But the Lord said to him, "Not so; anyone who kills Cain will suffer vengeance seven times over." Then the Lord put a mark on Cain so that no one who found him would kill him (Genesis 4: 1-15).

Joseph said: *Now Joseph had been taken down to Egypt. Potiphar, an Egyptian who was one of Pharaoh's officials, the captain of the guard, bought him from the Ishmaelite's who had taken him there. The Lord was with Joseph so that he prospered, and he lived in the house of his Egyptian master. When his master saw that the Lord was with him and that the Lord gave him success in everything he did, Joseph found favour in his eyes and became his attendant. Potiphar put him in charge of his household and he entrusted to his care everything he owned. From the time he put him in charge of his household and of all that he owned, the Lord blessed the household of the Egyptian because of Joseph. The blessing of the Lord was on everything Potiphar had, both in the house and in the field. So Potiphar left everything he had in Joseph's care; with Joseph in charge, he did not concern himself with anything except the food he ate.*

Now Joseph was well-built and handsome, and after a while his master's wife took notice of Joseph and said, "Come to bed with me!" But he refused. "With me in charge," he told her, "my master does not concern himself with anything in the house; everything he owns he has entrusted to my care. No one is greater in this house than I am. My master has withheld nothing from me except you, because you are his wife. How then could I do such a wicked thing and sin against God?" And though she spoke to Joseph day after day, he refused to go to bed with her or even be with her.

One day he went into the house to attend to his duties, and none of the household servants was inside. She caught him by his cloak and said, "Come to bed with me!" But he left his cloak in her hand and ran out of the house. When she saw that he had left his cloak in her hand and had run out of the house, she called her household servants. "Look," she said to them, "this Hebrew has been brought to us to make sport of us! He came in here to sleep with me, but I screamed. When he heard me scream for help, he left his cloak beside me and ran out of the house." She kept his cloak beside her until his master came home. Then she told him this story: "That Hebrew slave you brought us came to me to make sport of me. But as soon as I screamed for help, he left his cloak beside me and ran out of the house" (Genesis 39:4-18).

12. **Absence and Permission:**
The value you place on your job is what causes you to seek permission to be absent or call in when you are running late.

13. Your provable value is based on your manifestation of your assignment, which initiates your promotion.

14. Value creates attraction and admiration:
It directs focus, eliminates distraction, enforces determination, continuity persuasion, and comes with commitment, dedication and celebration. What you value, you will promote.

Who then is the one who condemns? No one. Christ Jesus who died—more than that, who was raised to life—is at the right hand of God and is also interceding for us. Who shall separate us from the love of Christ? Shall trouble or hardship or persecution or famine or nakedness or danger or sword? As it is written "For your sake we face death all day long; we are considered as sheep to be slaughtered." No, in all these things we are more than conquerors through him who loved us. For I am convinced that neither death nor life, neither angels nor demons, neither the present nor the future, nor any powers, neither height nor depth, nor anything else in all creation, will be able to separate us from the love of God that is in Christ Jesus our Lord (Romans 8:34-39).

But whatever were gains to me I now consider loss for the sake of Christ. What is more, I consider everything a loss because of the surpassing worth of knowing Christ Jesus my Lord, for whose sake I have lost all things. I consider them garbage, that I may gain Christ and be found in him, not having a righteousness of my own that comes from the law, but that which is through faith in Christ—the righteousness that comes from God on the basis of faith. I want to know Christ—yes, to know the power of his resurrection and participation in his sufferings, becoming like him in his death, and so, somehow, attaining to the resurrection from the dead. Not that I have already obtained all this, or have already arrived at my goal, but I press on to take hold of that for which Christ Jesus took hold of me.

Brothers and sisters, I do not consider myself yet to have taken hold of it. But one thing I do: Forgetting what is behind and straining toward what is ahead, I press on toward the goal to win the prize for which God has called me heavenward in Christ Jesus (Philippians 3:7-14).

But Daniel resolved not to defile himself with the royal food and wine, and he asked the chief official for permission not to defile himself this way. Now God had caused the official to show favour and compassion to Daniel, but the official told Daniel, "I am afraid of my lord the king, who has assigned your food and drink. Why should he see you looking worse than the other young men your age? The king would then have my head because of you."

Daniel then said to the guard whom the chief official had appointed over Daniel, Hananiah, Mishael and Azariah, "Please test your servants for ten days: Give us nothing but vegetables to eat and water to drink. Then compare our appearance with that of the young men who eat the royal food, and treat your servants in accordance with what you see." So he agreed to this and tested them for ten days (Daniel 1:8-14).

At this time some astrologers came forward and denounced the Jews. They said to King Nebuchadnezzar, "May the king live forever! Your Majesty has issued a decree that everyone who hears the sound of the horn, flute, zither, lyre, harp, pipe and all kinds of music must fall down and worship the image of gold, and that whoever does not fall down and worship will be thrown into a blazing furnace. But, there are some Jews whom you have set over the affairs of the province of Babylon—Shadrach, Meshach and Abednego—who pay no attention to you, your Majesty; they neither serve your gods nor worship the image of gold you have set up." Furious with rage, Nebuchadnezzar summoned Shadrach, Meshach and Abednego. So these men were brought before the king, and Nebuchadnezzar said to them, "Is it true, Shadrach, Meshach and Abednego, that you do not serve my gods or worship the image of gold I have set up? Now when you hear the sound of the horn, flute, zither, lyre, harp, pipe and all kinds of music, if you are ready to fall down and worship the image I made, very good. But if you do not worship it, you will be thrown immediately into a blazing furnace. Then what god will be able to rescue you from my hand?"

Shadrach, Meshach and Abednego replied to him, "King Nebuchadnezzar, we do not need to defend ourselves before you in this matter. If we are thrown into the blazing furnace, the God we serve is able to deliver us from it, and he will deliver us from Your Majesty's hand. But even if he does not, we want you to know, Your Majesty that we will not serve your gods or worship the image of gold you have set up." Then Nebuchadnezzar was furious with Shadrach, Meshach and Abednego, and his attitude toward them changed. He ordered the furnace heated seven times hotter than usual and commanded some of the strongest soldiers in his army to tie up Shadrach, Meshach and Abednego and throw them into the blazing furnace.

So these men, wearing their robes, trousers, turbans and other clothes, were bound and thrown into the blazing furnace. The king's command was so urgent and the furnace so hot that the flames of the fire killed the soldiers who took up Shadrach, Meshach and Abednego, and these three men, firmly tied, fell into the blazing furnace. Then King Nebuchadnezzar leaped to his feet in amazement and asked his advisers "Weren't there three men that we tied up and threw into the fire?" They replied, "Certainly, You're Majesty." He said, "Look! I see four men walking around in the fire, unbound and unharmed, and the fourth looks like a son of the gods." Nebuchadnezzar then approached the opening of the blazing furnace and shouted, "Shadrach, Meshach and Abednego, servants of the Most High God, come out! Come here!"

So Shadrach, Meshach and Abednego came out of the fire, and the satraps, prefects, governors and royal advisers crowded around them. They saw that the fire had not harmed their bodies, nor was a hair of their heads singed; their robes were not scorched, and there was no smell of fire on them. Then Nebuchadnezzar said, "Praise be to the God of Shadrach, Meshach and Abednego, who has sent his angel and rescued his servants! They trusted in him and defied the king's command and were willing to give up their lives rather than serve or worship any god except their own God. Therefore I decree that the people of any nation or language who say anything against the God of Shadrach, Meshach and Abednego be cut into pieces and their houses be turned into piles of rubble, for no other god can save in this way." Then the king promoted Shadrach, Meshach and Abednego in the province of Babylon (Daniel 3: 8 – 30).

It pleased Darius to appoint 120 satraps to rule throughout the kingdom, with three administrators over them, one of whom was Daniel. The satraps were made accountable to them so that the king might not suffer loss. Now Daniel so distinguished himself among the administrators and the satraps by his exceptional qualities that the king planned to set him over the whole kingdom. At this, the administrators and the satraps tried to find grounds for charges against Daniel in his conduct of government affairs, but they were unable to do so. They could find no corruption in him, because he was trustworthy and neither corrupt nor negligent. Finally these men said, "We will never find any basis for charges against this man Daniel unless it has something to do with the law of his God." So these administrators and satraps went as a group to the king and said: "May King Darius live forever! The royal administrators, prefects, satraps, advisers and governors have all agreed that the king should issue an edict and enforce the decree that anyone who prays to any god or human being during the next thirty days, except to you, Your Majesty, shall be thrown into the lions' den. Now, Your Majesty, issue the decree and put it in writing so that it cannot be altered—in accordance with the law of the Medes and Persians, which cannot be repealed."

So King Darius put the decree in writing. Now when Daniel learned that the decree had been published, he went home to his upstairs room where the windows opened toward Jerusalem. Three times a day he got down on his knees and prayed, giving thanks to his God, just as he had done before. Then these men went as a group and found Daniel praying and asking God for help. So they went to the king and spoke to him about his royal decree: "Did you not publish a decree that during the next thirty days anyone who prays to any god or human being except to you, Your Majesty, would be thrown into the lions' den?"
The king answered, "The decree stands—in accordance with the law of the Medes and Persians, which cannot be repealed." Then they said to the king, "Daniel, who is one of the exiles from Judah, pays no attention to you, Your Majesty, or to the decree you put in writing. He still prays three times a day." When the king heard this, he was greatly distressed; he was determined to rescue Daniel and made every effort until sundown to save him. Then the men went as a group to King Darius and said to him, "Remember, Your Majesty, that according to the law of the Medes and Persians no decree or edict that the king issues can be changed." So the king gave the order, and they brought Daniel and threw him into the lions' den. The king said to Daniel, "May your God, whom you serve continually, rescue you!" A stone was brought and placed over the mouth of the den, and the king sealed it with his own signet ring and with the rings of his nobles, so that Daniel's situation might not be changed.

Then the king returned to his palace and spent the night without eating and without any entertainment being brought to him. And he could not sleep. At the first light of dawn, the king got up and hurried to the lions' den. When he came near the den, he called to Daniel in an anguished voice, "Daniel, servant of the living God, has your God, whom you serve continually, been able to rescue you from the lions?" Daniel answered, "May the king live forever! My God sent his angel and he shut the mouths of the lions. They have not hurt me, because I was found innocent in his sight. Nor have I ever done any wrong before you, Your Majesty." The king was overjoyed and gave orders to lift Daniel out of the den. And when Daniel was lifted from the den, no wound was found on him, because he had trusted in his God. At the king's command, the men who had falsely accused Daniel were brought in and thrown into the lions' den, along with their wives and children. And before they reached the floor of the den, the lions overpowered them and crushed all their bones. Then King Darius wrote to all the nations and peoples of every language in all the earth: "May you prosper greatly! "I issue a decree that in every part of my kingdom people must fear and reverence the God of Daniel. "For he is the living God and he endures forever his kingdom will not be destroyed, his dominion will never end. He rescues and he saves, he performs signs and wonders in the heavens and on the earth. He has rescued Daniel from the power of the lions." So Daniel prospered during the reign of Darius and the reign of Cyrus, the Persian (Daniel 6:1-28).

15.   Ignorance:

People neglect value because of ignorance (Hosea 4:6). The enemies of the cross neglect good values. They neglect Christ and reach out to demon and choose them as their master because of ignorance and wickedness.

16.   Value demands accountability, submission, communication, order, attention, hard work, sacrifice, excellence and respect.

17.   God created man for woman, and woman for man because of value. Value initiates care, compassion, giving and love. So the man gave names to all the livestock, the birds in the sky and all the wild animals.

But for Adam no suitable helper was found. So the Lord God caused the man to fall into a deep sleep; and while he was sleeping, he took one of the man's ribs and then closed up the place with flesh. Then the Lord God made a woman from the rib he had taken out of the man, and he brought her to the man. The man said "This is now bone of my bones and flesh of my flesh; she shall be called 'woman, for she was taken out of man." That is why a man leaves his father and mother and is united to his wife, and they become one flesh. Adam and his wife were both naked, and they felt no shame. (Genesis 2:20-25).

∼

Chapter Three
IMPROVING YOUR ORGANISATION'S VALUES

1. Promoting your organisation or church through positive words. Avoid speaking words that can cause damage. Your words should be excellent and positive, thus having ability to promote your organisation or church in order to initiate growth and expansion. Use selected words that can be attractive and admirable to the public and people within your church or organisation. Defend your church or organisation with positive words and actions. We must remember that God has ownership of the church and Christ is the head of His church, therefore any negative words you say against the church affects God. Any attempt made by anyone to destroy the church by words or actions would hold you in contempt and would be destroying yourself.

Don't you know that you yourselves are God's temple and that God's Spirit dwells in your midst? If anyone destroys God's temple, God will destroy that person; for God's temple is sacred, and you together are that temple (1 Corinthians 3:16-17).

Many believers have misconceptions about church and its building and believe the building makes the church. But rather we as believers of Christ are the church and the church's building is the place of our meeting to worship and fellowship.

The church is a living organism; she lives and grows through living and positive words.

Then what if you see the Son of Man ascend to where he was before (John 6:62). *Negative words kills lives and we must avoid it because it might kill one before they know it. The tongue has the power of life and death, and those who love it will eat its fruit* (Proverbs 18:21). *The wise woman builds her house but, with her own hands the foolish one tears hers down. Whoever fears the Lord walks uprightly but, those who despise him are devious in their ways* (Proverbs 14:1-2).

2.   Overpower your weaknesses and failures by releasing your strengths. The devil can use a person weakness to destroy an organisation or church, because your weakness can be the area of your limitation. To prevent the evil of weakness, you should release your strength thus operating in it, whilst working on your weaknesses through prayer and the word. As you work in your church and organisation, you should recognise your weakness and avoid it.

Do not emphasise on your church's weaknesses internally or externally. It is evil to tell people outside your church what its weaknesses are, instead of emphasising on the strengths and all the good things the church is doing. Do not leave the church and return to see how bad it is doing. Do not make little comment such as, 'The pastor cannot speak good English' or 'The pastor's wife cannot pray well'. That is an evil thing to do. Speak well of the church, of the living God, and help find solutions to its problems.

Jesus overcame his weakness through the word of God after fasted. Jesus, full of the Holy Spirit, left the Jordan and was led by the Spirit into the wilderness, where for forty days he was tempted by the devil. He ate nothing during those days, and at the end of them he was hungry. The devil said to him, "If you are the Son of God, tell this stone to become bread." Jesus answered, "It is written: 'Man shall not live on bread alone.' The devil led him up to a high place and showed him in an instant all the kingdoms of the world. And he said to him, "I will give you all their authority and splendour; it has been given to me, and I can give it to anyone I want to. If you worship me, it will all be yours." Jesus answered, "It is written: 'Worship the Lord your God and serve him only.' The devil led him to Jerusalem and had him stand on the highest point of the temple. "If you are the Son of God," he said, "throw yourself down from here. For it is written: 'He will command his angels concerning you to guard you carefully; they will lift you up in their hands, so that you will not strike your foot against a stone.' Jesus answered, "It is said: 'Do not put the Lord your God to the test.' When the devil had finished all this tempting, he left him until an opportune time. Jesus Rejected at Nazareth. Jesus returned to Galilee in the power of the Spirit and news about him spread through the whole countryside (Luke 4:1-14).

Jesus released His strength through the word of God and overcame His weakness through the weapon of the word of God; therefore we are also instructed to be strong.

Finally, be strong in the Lord and in his mighty power (Ephesians 6:10).

3. **Presentation:** You should be careful in presenting your church to the public. Your presentation should be encouraging and enforcing people to be attracted to your church. Present your church in a positive and smart way, creating elements of attraction and admiration.

4. **Communication:** Do not communicate your product, church or organisation with an attitude of dullness, frustration or depression, but rather with an active force of attraction and good testimonies. You will communicate whatever you value.

At the end of forty days they returned from exploring the land. They came back to Moses and Aaron and the whole Israelite community at Kadesh in the Desert of Paran. There they reported to them and to the whole assembly and showed them the fruit of the land. They gave Moses this account: "We went into the land to which you sent us, and it does flow with milk and honey! Here is its fruit. But the people who live there are powerful, and the cities are fortified and very large. We even saw descendants of Anak there. The Amalekites live in the Negev; the Hittites, Jebusites and Amorites live in the hill country; and the

Canaanites live near the sea and along the Jordan." Then Caleb silenced the people before Moses and said, "We should go up and take possession of the land, for we can certainly do it." But the men who had gone up with him said, "We can't attack those people; they are stronger than we are." And they spread among the Israelites a bad report about the land they had explored. They said, "The land we explored devours those living in it. All the people we saw there are of great size. We saw the Nephilim there (the descendants of Anak come from the Nephilim). We seemed like grasshoppers in our own eyes, and we looked the same to them" (Numbers 13:25-33).

That night all the members of the community raised their voices and wept aloud. All the Israelites grumbled against Moses and Aaron, and the whole assembly said to them, "If only we had died in Egypt! Or in this wilderness! Why is the Lord bringing us to this land only to let us fall by the sword? Our wives and children will be taken as plunder. Wouldn't it be better for us to go back to Egypt?" And they said to each other, "We should choose a leader and go back to Egypt." Then Moses and Aaron fell face down in front of the whole Israelite assembly gathered there. Joshua son of Nun and Caleb son of Jephunneh, who were among those who had explored the land, tore their clothes and said to the entire Israelite assembly, "The land we passed through and explored is exceedingly good. If the Lord is pleased with us, he will lead us into that land, a land flowing with milk and honey, and will give it to us. Only do not rebel against the Lord. And do not be afraid of the people of the land, because we will devour them. Their protection is gone, but the Lord is with us. Do not be afraid of them." But the whole assembly talked about stoning them. Then the glory of the Lord appeared at the tent of meeting to all the Israelites. The Lord said to Moses, "How long will these people treat me with contempt? How long will they refuse to believe in me, in spite of all the signs I have performed among them? I will strike them down with a plague and destroy them, but I will make you into a nation greater and stronger than they." Moses said to the Lord, "Then the Egyptians will hear about it! By your power you brought these people up from among them. And they will tell the inhabitants of this land about it. They have already heard that you, Lord, are with these people and that you, Lord, have been seen face to face, that your cloud stays over them, and that you go before them in a pillar of cloud by day and a pillar of fire by night. If you put all these people to death, leaving none alive, the nations who have heard this report about you will say, 'The Lord was not able to bring these people into the land he promised them on oath, so he slaughtered them in the wilderness.' "Now may the Lord's strength be displayed, just as you have declared: 'The Lord is slow to anger, abounding in love and forgiving sin and rebellion? Yet he does not leave the guilty unpunished; he punishes the children for the sin of the parents to the third and fourth generation.' In accordance with your great love, forgive the sin of these people, just as you have pardoned them from the time they left Egypt until now." The Lord replied, "I have forgiven them, as you asked. Nevertheless, as surely as I live and as surely as the glory of the Lord fills the whole earth, not one of those who saw my glory and the signs I performed in Egypt and in the wilderness but who disobeyed me and tested me ten times— not one of them will ever see the land I promised on oath to their ancestors. No one who has treated me with contempt will ever see it. But because my servant Caleb has a different spirit and follows me wholeheartedly, I will bring him into the land he went to, and his descendants will inherit it. Since the Amalekites and the Canaanites are living in the valleys, turn back tomorrow and set out toward the desert along the route to the Red Sea." The Lord said to Moses and Aaron: "How long will this wicked community grumble against me? I have heard the complaints of these grumbling Israelites. So tell them, 'As surely as I live, declares the Lord, I will do to you the very thing I heard you say: In this wilderness your bodies will fall—every one of you twenty years old or more who was counted in the census and who has grumbled against me. Not one of you will enter the land I swore with uplifted hand to make your home, except Caleb son of Jephunneh and Joshua son of Nun. As for your children that you said would be taken as plunder, I will bring them in to enjoy the land you have rejected. But as for you, your bodies will fall in this wilderness. Your children will be shepherds here for forty years, suffering for your unfaithfulness, until the last of your bodies lies in the wilderness. For forty years—one year for each of the forty days you explored the land—you will suffer for your sins and know what it is like to have me against you.' I, the Lord, have spoken, and I will surely do these things to this whole wicked community, which has banded together against me. They will meet their end in this wilderness; here they will die." So the men Moses had sent to explore the land, who returned and made the whole community grumble against him by spreading a bad report about it— these men who were responsible for spreading the bad report about the land were struck down and died of a plague before the Lord. Of the men who went to explore the land, only Joshua son of Nun and Caleb son of Jephunneh survived. When Moses reported this to all the Israelites, they mourned bitterly. Early the next morning they set out for the highest point in the hill country, saying, "Now we are ready to go up to the land the Lord promised. Surely we have sinned!" But Moses said, "Why are you disobeying the Lord's command? This will not succeed! Do not go up, because the Lord is not with you. You will be defeated by your enemies, for the Amalekites and the Canaanites will face you there. Because you have turned away from the Lord, he will not be with you and you will fall by the sword." Nevertheless, in their presumption they went up toward the highest point in the hill country, though neither Moses nor the ark of the Lord's covenant moved from the camp. Then the Amalekites and the Canaanites who lived in that hill country came down and attacked them and beat them down all the way to Hormah (Numbers 14:1-45).

5. **Remind yourself about the enemies you must fight against.** The enemies may progress because their evil expectation is to see church and organisation fail. An individual may fail, but the word of God never fails and God wants us to succeed in everything. You must put on the whole armour of God to war against the thief and defend the value of your church and organisation.

But when Sanballat, Tobiah, the Arabs, the Ammonites and the people of Ashdod heard that the repairs to Jerusalem's walls had gone ahead and that the gaps were being closed, they were very angry. They all plotted together to come and fight against Jerusalem and stir up trouble against it. But we prayed to our God and posted a guard day and night to meet this threat. Meanwhile, the people in Judah said, "The strength of the labourers is giving out, and there is so much rubble that we cannot rebuild the wall." Also our enemies said, "Before they know it or see us, we will be right there among them and will kill them and put an end to the work." Then the Jews who lived near them came and told us ten times over, "Wherever you turn, they will attack us." Therefore I stationed some of the people behind the lowest points of the wall at the exposed places, posting them by families, with their swords, spears and bows. After I looked things over, I stood up and said to the nobles, the officials and the rest of the people "Don't be afraid of them. Remember the Lord, who is great and awesome, and fight for your families, your sons and your daughters, your wives and your homes." When our enemies heard that we were aware of their plot and that God had frustrated it, we all returned to the wall, each to our own work. From that day on, half of my men did the work, while the other half were equipped with spears, shields, bows and armour. The officers posted themselves behind all the people of Judah who were building the wall. Those who carried materials did their work with one hand and held a weapon in the other, and each of the builders wore his sword at his side as he worked. But the man who sounded the trumpet stayed with me. Then I said to the nobles, the officials and the rest of the people, "The work is extensive and spread out, and we are widely separated from each other along the wall. Wherever you hear the sound of the trumpet, join us there. Our God will fight for us!" So we continued the work with half the men holding spears, from the first light of dawn till the stars came out. At that time I also said to the people, "Have every man and his helper stay inside Jerusalem at night, so they can serve us as guards by night and as workers by day." Neither I nor my brothers nor my men nor the guards with me took off our clothes; each had his weapon, even when he went for water (Nehemiah 4: 7-23).

Jesus told them another parable: "The kingdom of heaven is like a man who sowed good seed in his field. But while everyone was sleeping, his enemy came and sowed weeds among the wheat, and went away. When the wheat sprouted and formed heads, then the weeds also appeared. "The owner's servants came to him and said, 'Sir, didn't you sow good seed in your field? Where then did the weeds come from?' "'An enemy did this,' he replied. "The servants asked him, 'Do you want us to go and pull them up?' 'No,' he answered, 'because while you are pulling the weeds, you may uproot the wheat with them. Let both grow together until the harvest. At that time I will tell the harvesters: First collect the weeds and tie them in bundles to be burned; then gather the wheat and bring it into my barn," (Matthew 13:24-30).

Finally, be strong in the Lord and in his mighty power. Put on the full armour of God, so that you can take your stand against the devil's schemes. For our struggle is not against flesh and blood, but against the rulers, against the authorities, against the powers of this dark world and against the spiritual forces of evil in the heavenly realms. Therefore put on the full armour of God, so that when the day of evil comes, you may be able to stand your ground, and after you have done everything, to stand. Stand firm then, with the belt of truth buckled around your waist, with the breastplate of righteousness in place, and with your feet fitted with the readiness that comes from the gospel of peace. In addition to all this, take up the shield of faith, with which you can extinguish all the flaming arrows of the evil one. Take the helmet of salvation and the sword of the Spirit, which is the word of God (Ephesians 6:10-17).

The thief comes only to steal and kill and destroy; I have come that they may have life, and have it to the full (John 10:10). Develop hatred against such enemies if you value your faith and also want to add value.

6.   We should develop an attitude of going forward, not backwards. We must refuse to be crushed and not allow anything to distract us. We should have an attitude of perseverance, never giving up, possibilities and positive results.

7.   Celebrate: You should be a celebrator of God and your church. Whatever you celebrate is loved; refuse to celebrate hate. Initiate the beauty of God and your church. Be a builder, not a destroyer.

The wise woman builds her house, but with her own hands the foolish one tear hers down. Whoever fears the Lord walks uprightly, but those who despise him are devious in their ways (Proverbs 14:1-2).

Address your church with good testimonies and be committed to its advantages for growth and expansion. Do not retire your church but rather relaunch, recommission and refine it.

8.   **Solution Mentality:** It is open revelation that solution is better than problem. It is good for us as believers in Christ to develop mentality of solutions. We should be seeking for solutions whenever problems appear. There are many wicked people who glory in problems rather than in solution. We are not born to be problem carriers, but solution givers, because we are born to win. Some people in the church thrive on problems however; this is not supposed to be so. Whenever there is a problem, some Christian's phones will be in action. They are doing themselves harm when people are gossiping about the church because the devil has no power over the church. The church should come together in this end time and focus on solutions for the Kingdom of God, instead of focusing on the problems.

Chapter Four
PROMOTING CHURCH VALUE

Value has the power to command respect and honour. Every church is preserved and protected by value. Value is also the crown of good image when the image of church is destroyed by forces of perversion and neglected by ignorance. It becomes stage for satanic manipulation, and the purpose of church or organisation will lose value. Loss of value is loss of glory, and value retained is glory retained.

The Lord said to Moses, "Send some men to explore the land of Canaan, which I am giving to the Israelites. From each ancestral tribe send one of its leaders." So at the Lord's command Moses sent them out from the Desert of Paran. All of them were leaders of the Israelites. These are their names: from the tribe of Reuben, Shammua son of Zakkur; from the tribe of Simeon, Shaphat son of Hori; from the tribe of Judah, Caleb son of Jephunneh; from the tribe of Issachar, Igal son of Joseph; from the tribe of Ephraim, Hoshea son of Nun; from the tribe of Benjamin, Palti son of Raphu; from the tribe of Zebulun, Gaddiel son of Sodi; from the tribe of Manasseh (a tribe of Joseph), Gaddi son of Susi; from the tribe of Dan, Ammiel son of Gemalli; from the tribe of Asher, Sethur son of Michael; from the tribe of Naphtali, Nahbi son of Vophsi from the tribe of Gad, Geuel son of Maki. These are the names of the men this land about it. They have already heard that you, Lord, are with these people and that you, Lord, have been seen face to face, that your cloud stays over them, and that you go before them in a pillar of cloud by day and a pillar of fire by night. If you put all these people to death, leaving none alive, the nations who have heard this report about you will say, 'The Lord was not able to bring these people into the land he promised them on oath, so he slaughtered them in the wilderness.' "Now may the Lord's strength be displayed, just as you have declared: 'The Lord is slow to anger, abounding in love and forgiving sin and rebellion? Yet he does not leave the guilty unpunished; he punishes the children for the sin of the parents to the third and fourth generation.' In accordance with your great love, forgive the sin of these people, just as you have pardoned them from the time they left Egypt until now." The Lord replied, "I have forgiven them, as you asked. Nevertheless, as surely as I live and as surely as the glory of the Lord fills the whole earth, not one of those who saw my glory and the signs I performed in Egypt and in the wilderness but who disobeyed me and tested me ten times— not one of them will ever see the land I promised on oath to their ancestors. No one who has treated me with contempt will ever see it. But because my servant Caleb has a different spirit and follows me wholeheartedly, I will bring him into the land he went to, and his descendants will inherit it. Since the Amalekites and the Canaanites are living in the valleys, turn back tomorrow and set out toward the desert along the route to the Red Sea." The Lord said to Moses and Aaron: "How long these will wicked community grumble against me? I have heard the complaints of these grumbling Israelites. So tell them, 'As surely as I live, declares the Lord, I will do to you the very thing I heard you say: In this wilderness your bodies will fall—every one of you twenty years old or more who was counted in the census and who has grumbled against me. Not one of you will enter the land I swore with uplifted hand to make your home, except Caleb son of Jephunneh and Joshua son of Nun. As for your children that you said would be taken as plunder, I will bring them in to enjoy the land you have rejected. But as for you, your bodies will fall in this wilderness. Your children will be shepherds here for forty years, suffering for your unfaithfulness, until the last of your bodies lies in the wilderness. For forty years—one year for each of the forty days you explored the land—you will suffer for your sins and know what it is like to have me against you.' I, the Lord, have spoken, and I will surely do these things to this whole wicked community, which has banded together against me. They will meet their end in this wilderness; here they will die." So the men Moses had sent to explore the land, who returned and made the whole community grumble against him by spreading a bad report about it— these men who were responsible for spreading the bad report about the land were struck down and died of a plague before the Lord. Of the men who went to explore the land, only Joshua son of Nun and Caleb son of Jephunneh survived. When Moses reported this to all the Israelites, they mourned bitterly. Early the next morning they set out for the highest point in the hill country, saying, "Now we are ready to go up to the land the Lord promised. Surely we have sinned!" But Moses said, "Why are you disobeying the Lord's command? This will not succeed! Do not go up, because the Lord is not with you. You will be defeated by your enemies, for the Amalekites and the Canaanites will face you there. Because you have turned away from the Lord, he will not be with you and you will fall by the sword." Nevertheless, in their presumption they went up toward the highest point in the hill country, though neither Moses nor the ark of the Lord's covenant moved from the camp. Then the Amalekites and the Canaanites who lived in that hill country came down and attacked them and beat them down all the way to Hormah (Numbers 14).

A. **Good Image:** *He has made everything beautiful in its time. He has also set eternity in the human heart; yet[a] no one can fathom what God has done from beginning to end* (Ecclesiastes 3:11).

B. **Good Report:** *They gave Moses this account: "We went into the land to which you sent us, and it does flow with milk and honey! Here is its fruit. But the people who live there are powerful and the cities are fortified and very large. We even saw descendants of Anak there. The Amalekites live in the Negev; the Hittites, Jebusites and Amorites live in the hill country; and the Canaanites live near the sea and along the Jordan." Then Caleb silenced the people before Moses and said, "We should go up and take possession of the land, for we can certainly do it." But the men who had gone up with him said, "We can't attack those people; they are stronger than we are." And they spread among the Israelites a bad report about the land they had explored. They said, "The land we explored devours those living in it. All the people we saw there are of great size. We saw the Nephilim there (the descendants of Anak come from the Nephilim). We seemed* *like grasshoppers in our own eyes, and we looked the same to them"* (Numbers 13:27-33).

C. **Good Advertisement:** *The Lord said to Moses and Aaron: 'Take a census of the Kohathite branch of the Levites by their clans and families. Count all the men from thirty to fifty years of age who come to serve in the work at the tent of meeting. This is the work of the Kohathites at the tent of meeting: the care of the most holy things. When the camp is to move, Aaron and his sons are to go in and take down the shielding curtain and put it over the Ark of the Covenant law. Then they are to cover the curtain with a durable leather, spread a cloth of solid blue over that and put the poles in place. Over the table of the Presence they are to spread a blue cloth and put on it the plates, dishes and bowls, and the jars for drink offerings; the bread that is continually there is to remain on it. They are to spread a scarlet cloth over them, cover that with the durable leather and put the poles in place. "Hey are to take a blue cloth and cover the lamp stand that is for light, together with its lamps, its wick trimmers and trays, and all its jars for the olive oil used to supply it. Then they are to wrap it and all its accessories in a covering of the durable leather and put it on a carrying frame'* (Numbers 4:1-10).

D. **Good Testimony:**

Jacob's well was there, and Jesus, tired as he was from the journey, sat down by the well. It was about noon. When a Samaritan woman came to draw water, Jesus said to her, "Will you give me a drink?" (His disciples had gone into the town to buy food.) The Samaritan woman said to him, "You are a Jew and I am a Samaritan woman. How can you ask me for a drink?" (For Jews do not associate with Samaritans). Jesus answered her, "If you knew the gift of God and who it is that asks you for a drink, you would have asked him and he would have given you living water." "Sir," the woman said, "you have nothing to draw with and the well is deep. Where can you get this living water? Are you greater than our father Jacob, who gave us the well and drank from it himself, as did also his sons and his livestock?"

Jesus answered, "Everyone who drinks this water will be thirsty again, but whoever drinks the water I give them will never thirst. Indeed, the water I give them will become in them a spring of water welling up to eternal life." The woman said to him, "Sir, give me this water so that I won't get thirsty and have to keep coming here to draw water." He told her, "Go, call your husband and come back." "I have no husband," she replied.

Jesus said to her, "You are right when you say you have no husband. The fact is, you have had five husbands, and the man you now have is not your husband. What you have just said is quite true." "Sir," the woman said, "I can see that you are a prophet (John 4:6-19).

Many of the Samaritans from that town believed in him because of the woman's testimony, "He told me everything I ever did" So when the Samaritans came to him, they urged him to stay with them, and he stayed two days. And because of his words many more became believers. They said to the woman, "We no longer believe just because of what you said; now we have heard for ourselves, and we know that this man really is the Saviour of the world" (John 4:39-42).

A, B and C promote image in church; promoting good image of your church by speaking the right words, helps to avoid destroying the church because emphasis will be placed on the church's strengths instead of weaknesses. Where there may be weaknesses in the organisation of the church, such weaknesses should be internal matters to be dealt with and not external, because such weaknesses are subject to solutions. There is no perfect church; the head of the church is Christ and he will work to bring it to perfection. One cannot complain when a potter is moulding and making a person life.

Communication should be built instead of pulling it down. Communicate your church with positive attitude internally and externally. Avoid all manner of evil communication. Communication is a foundational way of building values of your church because we are witness of our church.

Whatever is said within the church or organisation can either build or pull them down. We should use our positive communication with positive attitudes to add value to our church. It will invite good aroma of conductive environment for growth and unity. This will help us to eliminate division and confusion. The church is current of life:

The tongue has the power of life and death, and those who love it will eat its fruit (Proverbs 18:21).

The hearts of the wise make their mouths prudent, and their lips promote instruction (Proverbs 16:23).

For by your words you will be acquitted and by your words you will be condemned (Matthew 12:37).

Do not go about spreading slander among your people. 'Do not do anything that endangers your neighbor's life. I am the Lord' (Leviticus19:16).

Positive words empower growth but negative words conceived and spoken hinders growth, initiate limitations and causes romantic evil that either scatter or prevent people from coming into church. Protect your church with wisdom and avoid foolish behaviours and ignorance.

Better a dry crust with peace and quiet than a house full of feasting, with strife. A prudent servant will rule over a disgraceful son and will share the inheritance as one of the family. The crucible for silver and the furnace for gold but the Lord tests the heart. A wicked person listens to deceitful lips; a liar pays attention to a destructive tongue. Whoever mocks the poor shows contempt for their Maker; whoever gloats over disaster will not go unpunished. Children's children are a crown to the aged, and parents are the pride of their children. Eloquent lips are unsuited to a godless fool— how much worse lying lips to a ruler! A bribe is seen as a charm by the one who gives it; they think success will come at every turn.

Whoever would foster love covers over an offense, but whoever repeats the matter separates close friends. A rebuke impresses a discerning person more than a hundred lashes a fool. Evildoers' foster rebellion against God, the messenger of death will be sent against them. Better to meet a bear robbed of her cubs than a fool bent on folly. Evil will never leave the house of one who pays back evil for good. Starting a quarrel is like breaching a dam; so drop the matter before a dispute breaks out. Acquitting the guilty and condemning the innocent—the Lord detests them both.

Why should fools have money in hand to buy wisdom, when they are not able to understand it? A friend loves at all times, and a brother is born for a time of adversity. One who has no sense shakes hands in pledge and puts up security for a neighbor.

Whoever loves a quarrel loves sin; whoever builds a high gate invites destruction. One whose heart is corrupt does not prosper; one whose tongue is perverse falls into trouble. To have a fool for a child brings grief; there is no joy for the parent of a godless fool.

A cheerful heart is good medicine, but a crushed spirit dries up the bones. The wicked accept bribes in secret to pervert the course of justice. A discerning person keeps wisdom in view, but a fool's eyes wander to the ends of the earth. A foolish son brings grief to his father and bitterness to the mother who bore him. If imposing a fine on the innocent is not good, surely to flog honest officials is not right. The one who has knowledge uses words with restraint, and whoever has understanding is even-tempered. Even fools are thought wise if they keep silent, and discerning if they hold their tongues (Proverbs 17:1-28).

A wise son brings joy to his father, but a foolish son brings grief to his mother (Proverbs 10:1).

The wise woman builds her house, but with her own hands the foolish one tears hers down. Whoever fears the Lord walks uprightly, but those who despise him are devious in their ways. A fool's mouth lashes out with pride, but the lips of the wise protect them. Where there are no oxen, the manger is empty, but from the strength of an ox come abundant harvests. An honest witness does not deceive, but a false witness pours out lies. The mocker seeks wisdom and finds none, but knowledge comes easily to the discerning. Stay away from a fool, for you will not find knowledge on their lips. The wisdom of the prudent is to give thought to their ways, but the folly of fools is deception. Fools mock at making amends for sin, but goodwill is found among the upright. Each heart knows its own bitterness, and no one else can share its joy. The house of the wicked will be destroyed, but the tent of the upright will flourish. There is a way that appears to be right, but in the end it leads to death. Even in laughter the heart may ache, and rejoicing may end in grief. The faithless will be fully repaid for their ways, and the good rewarded for theirs. The simple believe anything, but the prudent give thought to their steps. The wise fear the Lord and shun evil but a fool is hot headed and yet feels secure. A quick-tempered person does foolish things, and the one who devises evil schemes is hated. The simple inherit folly, but the prudent are crowned with knowledge. Evildoers will bow down in the presence of the good, and the wicked at the gates of the righteous. The poor are shunned even by their neighbours, but the rich have many friends. It is a sin to despise one's neighbour, but blessed is the one who is kind to the needy. Do not those who plot evil go astray? But those who plan what is good find[a] love and faithfulness. All hard work brings a profit, but mere talk leads only to poverty. The wealth of the wise is their crown, but the folly of fools yields folly. A truthful witness saves lives, but a false witness is deceitful. Whoever fears the Lord has a secure fortress, and for their children it will be a refuge. The fear of the Lord is a fountain of life, turning a person from the snares of death. A large population is a king's glory, but without subjects a prince is ruined. Whoever is patient has great understanding, but one who is quick-tempered displays folly. A heart at peace gives life to the body, but envy rots the bones. Whoever oppresses the poor shows contempt for their Maker, but whoever is kind to the needy honours God. When calamity comes, the wicked are brought down, but even in death the righteous seek refuge in God. Wisdom reposes in the heart of the discerning and even among fools she lets herself be known. Righteousness exalts a nation, but sin condemns any people. A king delights in a wise servant, but a shameful servant arouses his fury (Proverbs 14: 1- 35).

A gentle answer turns away wrath, but a harsh word stirs up anger. The tongue of the wise adorns knowledge, but the mouth of the fool gushes folly. The eyes of the Lord are everywhere, keeping watch on the wicked and the good. The soothing tongue is a tree of life, but a perverse tongue crushes the spirit. A fool spurns a parent's discipline, but whoever heeds correction shows prudence.

The house of the righteous contains great treasure, but the income of the wicked brings ruin. The lips of the wise spread knowledge, but the hearts of fools are not upright. The Lord detests the sacrifice of the wicked, but the prayer of the upright pleases him. The Lord detests the way of the wicked; but he loves those who pursue righteousness. Stern discipline awaits anyone who leaves the path; the one who hates correction will die. Death and Destruction lie open before the Lord—how much more do human hearts! Mockers resent correction, so they avoid the wise.

A happy heart makes the face cheerful, but heartache crushes the spirit. The discerning heart seeks knowledge, but the mouth of a fool feeds on folly. All the days of the oppressed are wretched, but the cheerful heart has a continual feast. Better a little with the fear of the Lord than great wealth with turmoil. Better a small serving of vegetables with love than a fattened calf with hatred. A hot-tempered person stirs up conflict, but the one who is patient calms a quarrel. The way of the sluggard is blocked with thorns, but the path of the upright is a highway. A wise son brings joy to his father, but a foolish man despises his mother. Folly brings joy to one who has no sense, but whoever has understanding keeps a straight course. Plans fail for lack of counsel, but with many advisers they succeed.

A person finds joy in giving an apt reply and how good is a timely word! The path of life leads upward for the prudent to keep them from going down to the realm of the dead. The Lord tears down the house of the proud, but he sets the widow's boundary stones in place. The Lord detests the thoughts of the wicked, but gracious words are pure in his sight. The greedy bring ruin to their households, but the one who hates bribes will live. The heart of the righteous weighs its answers, but the mouth of the wicked gushes evil. The Lord is far from the wicked, but he hears the prayer of the righteous. Light in a messenger's eyes brings joy to the heart, and good news gives health to the bones. Whoever heeds life-giving correction will be at home among the wise. Those who disregard discipline despise themselves, but the one who heeds correction gains understanding. Wisdom's instruction is to fear the Lord, and humility comes before honour (Proverbs 15:1-33).

Chapter Five
POWER OF VALUE

No one can serve two masters. Either you will hate the one and love the other, or you will be devoted to the one and despise the other. You cannot serve both God and money. "Therefore I tell you, do not worry about your life, what you will eat or drink; or about your body, what you will wear. Is not life more than food, and the body more than clothes? Look at the birds of the air; they do not sow or reap or store away in barns, and yet your heavenly Father feeds them. Are you not much more valuable than they? Can any one of you by worrying add a single hour to your life? "And why do you worry about clothes? See how the flowers of the field grow. They do not labour or spin. Yet I tell you that not even Solomon in all his splendour was dressed like one of these. If that is how God clothes the grass of the field, which is here today and tomorrow is thrown into the fire, will he not much more clothe you—you of little faith? So do not worry, saying, 'What shall we eat?' or 'What shall we drink?' or 'What shall we wear?' For the pagans run after all these things, and your heavenly Father knows that you need them. But seek first his kingdom and his righteousness, and all these things will be given to you as well. Therefore do not worry about tomorrow, for tomorrow will worry about itself. Each day has enough trouble of its own (Matthew 6:24-34).

The opposite scriptures show us clearly that faith and value eliminate fear, unbelief, doubts, worries and double mindedness. Faith in action builds confidence with the word of God, knowing in your mind and heart that God can be trusted. The proof of your faith is God's approval and promotion, and the value you place on faith triggers manifestations of your faith. Faithlessness is lack of faith value, for example the Bible talks about certain woman with the issue of blood. The problem had robbed her of identity, dignity and value; she was on scale of devaluation.

Application of Value

And a woman was there who had been subject to bleeding for twelve years. She had suffered a great deal under the care of many doctors and had spent all she had, yet instead of getting better she grew worse. When she heard about Jesus, she came up behind him in the crowd and touched his cloak, because she thought, "If I just touch his clothes, I will be healed." Immediately her bleeding stopped and she felt in her body that she was freed from her suffering. At once Jesus realized that power had gone out from him. He turned around in the crowd and asked, "Who touched my clothes?" "You see the people crowding against you," his disciples answered, "and yet you can ask, 'Who touched me?' But Jesus kept looking around to see who had done it. Then the woman, knowing what had happened to her, came and fell at his feet and, trembling with fear, told him the whole truth. He said to her, "Daughter, your faith has healed you. Go in peace and be freed from your suffering (Mark 5:25-34).

This woman placed high value on Jesus' ability to make her well. God heard her and the issue of blood ceased. What you value only works for you.

Double Values meaning law of two values are the following:

1. **Neglect of value:** Whatever you have neglected initiates separation.

2. **Discovery of value initiates recovery**

3. **Ignorance of value initiates destruction.** My people are destroyed for lack of knowledge. *Because you have rejected knowledge, I also reject you as my priests; because you have ignored the law of your God, I also will ignore your children* (Hosea 4:6).

4. **Passion for value initiates drive and pursuit.**

5. **Determination and risk due to value create dangerous effort.**

6. **Placement of priority:** What you value attracts first priority and effective and efficient attention. We respond to what we value.

7. **Misplacement of value initiates disappointment and hard labour.**

8. **Value motivates action and movement.** It generates energy and divine faith, not casual faith or law of probability because faith is not a concept of probability.

9. **Loss of value initiates loss of recovery drive and determination to reach out for recovery value.**

Watch out for false prophets. They come to you in sheep's clothing, but inwardly they are ferocious wolves. By their fruit you will recognize them. Do people pick grapes from thorn bushes, or figs from thistles? Likewise, every good tree bears good fruit, but a bad tree bears bad fruit. A good tree cannot bear bad fruit, and a bad tree cannot bear good fruit.

Every tree that does not bear good fruit is cut down and thrown into the fire. Thus, by their fruit you will recognize them. "Not everyone who says to me, 'Lord, Lord,' will enter the kingdom of heaven, but only the one who does the will of my Father who is in heaven. Many will say to me on that day, 'Lord, Lord, did we not prophesy in your name and in your name drive out demons and in your name perform many miracles?' Then I will tell them plainly, 'I never knew you. Away from me, you evildoers!' (Matthew 7:15-23).

Loss of value causes:

i. **Stagnation**
ii. **Emptiness in life**
iii. **Loss of vision**
iv. **Loss of birth and delivery**

Positive Value

Value is the fuel for positive attainments. Your engaging with things will define your value and result orientation.

Negative Value

Engaging on things without value is characterised by failure and defeat. There is no value in worrying. However, faith has value *therefore everyone who hears these words of mine and puts them into practice is like a wise man who built his house on the rock. The rain came down, the streams rose, and the winds blew and beat against that house; yet it did not fall, because it had its foundation on the rock. But everyone who hears these words of mine and does not put them into practice is like a foolish man who built his house on sand. The rain came down, the streams rose, and the winds blew and beat against that house, and it fell with a great crash.*

When Jesus had finished saying these things, the crowds were amazed at his teaching, because he taught as one who had authority, and not as their teachers of the law (Matthew 7:24-29). It is important to build on rock based on value of what he hears. He or she will be strong, solid and established on the word of God which is Christ.

1. Resistance was initiated

2. Failure and defeat were eliminated

3. Discovery of value and soaking with value makes wise men. *Leaving that place, Jesus withdrew to the region of Tyre and Sidon. A Canaanite woman from that vicinity came to him, crying out, "Lord, Son of David, have mercy on me! My daughter is demon-possessed and suffering terribly." Jesus did not answer a word. So his disciples came to him and urged him, "Send her away, for she keeps crying out after us." He answered, "I was sent only to the lost sheep of Israel." The woman came and knelt before him. "Lord, help me!" she said. He replied, "It is not right to take the children's bread and toss it to the dogs." "Yes it is, Lord," she said. "Even the dogs eat the crumbs that fall from their master's table." Then Jesus said to her, "Woman, you have great faith! Your request is granted." And her daughter was healed at that moment* (Matthew 15:21-28).

Neglect of Value

But everyone who hears these words of mine and does not put them into practice is like a foolish man who built his house on sand. The rain came down, the streams rose, and the winds blew and beat against that house, and it fell with a great crash. When Jesus had finished saying these things, the crowds were amazed at his teaching, because he taught as one who had authority, and not as their teachers of the law (Matthew 7:26-29).

Misplacement of value initiates disgrace. It initiates foolishness and absence of resistance, failure, defeat, shame and disgrace.

Your success is based on value and failure could be based on the following:

1. Misplacement of Value
2. Absence of Value
3. Negligence of Value
4. Ignorance of Value
5. Errors of Defective Values
6. Conflicting Values: No one can serve two masters. Either you will hate the one and love the other, or you will be devoted to the one and despise the other. You cannot serve both God and money (Matthew 6:24).
7. Lack of pursuit of value due to:
    a. Laziness

b. Procrastination

c. Low energy and lack or negative passion

d. Absence mindless, slothfulness and sluggishness

e. Absence of hearing and doing skills

But the seed falling on good soil refers to someone who hears the word and understands it. This is the one who produces a crop, yielding a hundred, sixty or thirty times what was sown (Matthew 13:23).

∼

So do not worry, saying,
'What shall we eat?' or
'What shall we drink?' or
'What shall we wear?'
For the pagans run after
all these things,
and your heavenly Father
knows that you need them.

Chapter Six
VALUE & FEAR OF GOD

When you value something, you respect and protect it. God assured us of His protection and divine security because he values us, as a father values his children. Absence of value brings lack of respect and honour. Disrespect and dishonour are birth of devaluation. Whatever you devaluate cannot work for you. Where there is devaluation, there is negligence. Whatever you neglect cannot function because it is retired or eliminated from functioning process and functioning capacity. It will remain until restored or reinstated to value level.

What I tell you in the dark, speak in the daylight; what is whispered in your ear, proclaim from the roofs. Do not be afraid of those who kill the body but cannot kill the soul. Rather, be afraid of the One who can destroy both soul and body in hell. Are not two sparrows sold for a penny? Yet not one of them will fall to the ground outside your Father's care. And even the very hairs of your head are all numbered. So don't be afraid; you are worth more than many sparrows. Whoever acknowledges me before others, I will also acknowledge before my Father in heaven. But whoever disowns me before others, I will disown before my Father in heaven. Do not suppose that I have come to bring peace to the earth. I did not come to bring peace, but a sword. For I have come to turn 'a man against his father, a daughter against her mother, a daughter-in-law against her mother-in-law— a man's enemies will be the members of his own household.' Anyone who loves their father or mother more than me is not worthy of me; anyone who loves their son or daughter more than me is not worthy of me. Whoever does not take up their cross and follow me is not worthy of me. Whoever finds their life will lose it, and whoever loses their life for my sake will find it. Anyone who welcomes you welcomes me, and anyone who welcomes me welcomes the one who sent me. Whoever welcomes a prophet as a prophet will receive a prophet's reward, and whoever welcomes a righteous person as a righteous person will receive a righteous person's reward. And if anyone gives even a cup of cold water to one of these little ones who is my disciple, truly I tell you, that person will certainly not lose their reward (Matthew 10:27-42).

No one can serve two masters. Either you will hate the one and love the other, or you will be devoted to the one and despise the other. You cannot serve both God and money. Therefore I tell you, do not worry about your life, what you will eat or drink; or about your body, what you will wear. Is not life more than food and the body more than clothes? Look at the birds of the air; they do not sow or reap or store away in barns, and yet your heavenly Father feeds them. Are you not much more valuable than they? Can any one of you by worrying add a single hour to your life?

And why do you worry about clothes? See how the flowers of the field grow. They do not labour or spin. Yet I tell you that not even Solomon in all his splendor was dressed like one of these. If that is how God clothes the grass of the field, which is here today and tomorrow is thrown into the fire, will he not much more clothe you—you of little faith? So do not worry, saying, 'What shall we eat?' or 'What shall we drink?' or 'What shall we wear?' For the pagans run after all these things, and your heavenly Father knows that you need them. But seek first his kingdom and his righteousness, and all these things will be given to you as well. Therefore do not worry about tomorrow, for tomorrow will worry about itself. Each day has enough trouble of its own (Matthew 6:24-34).

Intercessor vs. Value

I urge, then, first of all, that petitions, prayers, intercession and thanksgiving be made for all people— for kings and all those in authority, that we may live peaceful and quiet lives in all godliness and holiness. This is good, and pleases God our Saviour, who wants all people to be saved and to come to knowledge of the truth. For there is one God, and one mediator between God and mankind, the man Christ Jesus who gave himself as a ransom for all people. This has now been witnessed to at the proper time. And for this purpose I was appointed a herald and an apostle—I am telling the truth, I am not lying—and a true and faithful teacher of the Gentiles (1 Timothy 2:1-7).

If you are an intercessor, you value your pastor, church, leaders and nation, then you cannot talk about them maliciously, because you cannot kill what you want to keep alive when making petition on their behalf. You use a choice of words that shows you value them and you also recognise the value of your commission.

This is applicable to every other office or callings in the body of Christ. The fivefold ministry gifts are defined based on value. Jesus values the church and desires that the lost be saved, therefore he implements this effective and efficient organisation of fivefold ministry. Where there is no value, there is absence of effectiveness and efficiency. It also attracts procrastination, slothfulness, sluggishness, excuses and delay. Furthermore, it initiates depression and frustrates response.

But to each one of us grace has been given as Christ apportioned it. This is why it says: "When he ascended on high, he took many captives and gave gifts to his people." (What does "he ascended" mean except that he also descended to the lower, earthly regions? He who descended is the very one who ascended higher than all the heavens, in order to fill the whole universe). So Christ himself gave the apostles, the prophets, the evangelists, the pastors and teachers, to equip his people for works of service, so that the body of Christ may be built up until we all reach unity in the faith and in the knowledge of the Son of God and become mature, attaining to the whole measure of the fullness of Christ. Then we will no longer be infants, tossed back and forth by the waves, and blown here and there by every wind of teaching and by the cunning and craftiness of people in their deceitful scheming. Instead, speaking the truth in love, we will grow to become in every respect the mature body of him who is the head, that is, Christ. From him the whole body, joined and held together by every supporting ligament, grows and builds itself up in love, as each part does its work (Ephesians 4:7-16).

Values vs. Enjoyment

What we value, we enjoy doing and putting more effort to achieve success. Whatever we value has the following signs:

1. Strength
2. Effort
3. Determination is greatly involved
4. Pursuit and courage
5. Consistency
6. Persistence: it is said persistence breaks resistance
7. Time availability: you can create time for whatever you value and really desire
8. Protection: what we value we protect with all that is within us

Value helps to eliminate the following because they are the enemies of value:

1. Excuses
2. Delay-decay
3. Carelessness
4. Effortlessness
5. Procrastination
6. Sluggishness
7. Time wastage
8. Inconsistency
9. Fear
10. Unbelief
11. Doubt
12. Hindrance

Value and Passion

Jesus Christ came into this planet earth to promote the value of God and his will. *The Lord said to Moses, "Speak to the Israelites and say to them: 'I am the Lord your God. You must not do as they do in Egypt, where you used to live, and you must not do as they do in the land of Canaan, where I am bringing you. Do not follow their practices. You must obey my laws and be careful to follow my decrees. I am the Lord your God. Keep my decrees and* laws, for the person who obeys them will live by them. I am the Lord.

'No one is to approach any close relative to have sexual relations. I am the Lord.

'Do not dishonor your father by having sexual relations with your mother. She is your mother; do not have relations with her.

'Do not have sexual relations with your father's wife; that would dishonor your father.

'Do not have sexual relations with your sister, either your father's daughter or your mother's daughter, whether she was born in the same home or elsewhere.

'Do not have sexual relations with your son's daughter or your daughter's daughter; that would dishonour you.

'Do not have sexual relations with the daughter of your father's wife, born to your father; she is your sister.

'Do not have sexual relations with your father's sister; she is your father's close relative.

'Do not have sexual relations with your mother's sister, because she is your mother's close relative. 'Do not dishonour your father's brother by approaching his wife to have sexual relations; she is your aunt.

'Do not have sexual relations with your daughter-in-law. She is your son's wife; do not have relations with her."

'Do not have sexual relations with your brother's wife; that would dishonour your brother.

'Do not have sexual relations with both a woman and her daughter. Do not have sexual relations with either her son's daughter or her daughter's daughter; they are her close relatives. That is wickedness.

'Do not take your wife's sister as a rival wife and have sexual relations with her while your wife is living.

'Do not approach a woman to have sexual relations during the uncleanness of her monthly period.

'Do not have sexual relations with your neighbour's wife and defile yourself with her.

'Do not give any of your children to be sacrificed to Molek, for you must not profane the name of your God. I am the Lord. 'Do not have sexual relations with a man as one does with a woman; that is detestable.

'Do not have sexual relations with an animal and defile yourself with it. A woman must not present herself to an animal to have sexual relations with it; that is a perversion."

'Do not defile yourselves in any of these ways, because this is how the nations that I am going to drive out before you became defiled. Even the land was defiled; so I punished it for its sin, and the land vomited out its inhabitants.

But you must keep my decrees and my laws. The native-born and the foreigners residing among you must not do any of these detestable things, for all these things were done by the people who lived in the land before you, and the land became defiled. And if you defile the land, it will vomit you out as it vomited out the nations that were before you.

'Everyone who does any of these detestable things—such persons must be cut off from their people. Keep my requirements and do not follow any of the detestable customs that were practiced before you came and do not defile yourselves with them. I am the Lord your God" (Leviticus 18:1-30).'

"Woe to the obstinate children," declares the Lord, "to those who carry out plans that are not mine, forming an alliance, but not by my Spirit, heaping sin upon sin; who go down to Egypt without consulting me; who look for help to Pharaoh's protection, to Egypt's shade for refuge but Pharaoh's protection will be to your shame, Egypt's shade will bring you disgrace. Though they have officials in Zoan and their envoys have arrived in Hanes, everyone will be put to shame because of a people useless to them, who bring neither help nor advantage, but only shame and disgrace."

A prophecy concerning the animals of the Negev: Through a land of hardship and distress, of lions and lionesses, of adders and darting snakes, the envoys carry their riches on donkeys' backs, their treasures on the humps of camels, to that unprofitable nation, to Egypt, whose help is utterly useless. Therefore I call her Rahab the Do-Nothing. Go now, write it on a tablet for them, and inscribe it on a scroll, that for the days to come it may be an everlasting witness. For these are rebellious people, deceitful children; children unwilling to listen to the Lord's instruction. They say to the seers, "See no more visions!" and to the prophets, "Give us no more visions of what is right! Tell us pleasant things, prophesy illusions. Leave this way, get off this path, and stop confronting us with the Holy One of Israel!" Therefore this is what the Holy One of Israel says: "Because you have rejected this message, relied on oppression and depended on deceit, this sin will become for you like a high wall, cracked and bulging, that collapses suddenly, in an instant. It will break in pieces like pottery, shattered so merciless less that among its pieces not a fragment will be found for taking coals from a hearth or scooping water out of a cistern."

This is what the Sovereign Lord, the Holy One of Israel, says: "In repentance and rest is your salvation, in quietness and trust is your strength, but you would have none of it. You said, 'No, we will flee on horses.' Therefore you will flee! You said, 'We will ride off on swift horses.' Therefore your pursuers will be swift! A thousand will flee at the threat of one; at the threat of five you will all flee away, till you are left like a flagstaff on a mountaintop, like a banner on a hill." Yet the Lord longs to be gracious to you; therefore he will rise up to show you compassion.

For the Lord is a God of justice. Blessed are all who wait for him! People of Zion, who live in Jerusalem, you will weep no more. How gracious he will be when you cry for help! As soon as he hears, he will answer you. Although the Lord gives you the bread of adversity and the water of affliction, your teachers will be hidden no more; with your own eyes you will see them. Whether you turn to the right or to the left, your ears will hear a voice behind you, saying, "This is the way; walk in it." Then you will desecrate your idols overlaid with silver and your images covered with gold; you will throw them away like a menstrual cloth and say to them, "Away with you!"

He will also send you rain for the seed you sow in the ground, and the food that comes from the land will be rich and plentiful.

In that day your cattle will graze in broad meadows. The oxen and donkeys that work the soil will eat fodder and mash, spread out with fork and shovel. In the day of great slaughter, when the towers fall, streams of water will flow on every high mountain and every lofty hill. The moon will shine like the sun, and the sunlight will be seven times brighter, like the light of seven full days, when the Lord binds up the bruises of his people and heals the wounds he inflicted. See, the Name of the Lord comes from afar, with burning anger and dense clouds of smoke; his lips are full of wrath, and his tongue is a consuming fire.

His breath is like a rushing torrent, rising up to the neck. He shakes the nations in the sieve of destruction; he places in the jaws of the peoples a bit that leads them astray. And you will sing as on the night you celebrate a holy festival; your hearts will rejoice as when people playing pipes go up to the mountain of the Lord, to the Rock of Israel. The Lord will cause people to hear his majestic voice and will make them see his arm coming down with raging anger and consuming fire, with cloudburst, thunderstorm and hail. The voice of the Lord will shatter Assyria; with his rod he will strike them down. Every stroke the Lord lays on them with his punishing club will be to the music of timbrels and harps, as he fights them in battle with the blows of his arm. Topheth has long been prepared; it has been made ready for the king. Its fire pit has been made deep and wide, with an abundance of fire and wood; the breath of the Lord, like a stream of burning sulfur, sets it ablaze (Isaiah 30:1-33).

So don't be afraid; you are worth more than many sparrows (Matthew 10:31).

All the believers were together and had everything in common. They sold property and possessions to give to anyone who had need (Acts 2:44-45).

Jesus sat down opposite the place where the offerings were put and watched the crowd putting their money into the temple treasury. Many rich people threw in large amounts. But a poor widow came and put in two very small copper coins, worth only a few cents. Calling his disciples to him, Jesus said, "Truly I tell you, this poor widow has put more into the treasury than all the others. They all gave out of their wealth; but she, out of her poverty, put in everything—all she had to live on." (Mark 12:41-44).

For the sexually immoral, for those practicing homosexuality, for slave traders and liars and perjurers—and for whatever else is contrary to the sound doctrine (1 Timothy 1:10).

Wherever you are valued becomes a place of your strength. Wherever you are not valued weakens your strength and performance, your response to value and your productivity. Value can change insignificance to significance. It promotes growth and expansion. A place of value initiates promotion. Where value is respected and recognised, things work faster. Where there is no value, there is disgrace and things do not work well. Absence of value promotes insignificance, negative downfall and failure.

Efficiency and effectiveness are restricted in a place where values are not operating. *After the two days he left for Galilee. (Now Jesus himself had pointed out that a prophet has no honor in his own country). When he arrived in Galilee, the Galileans welcomed him. They had seen all that he had done in Jerusalem at the Passover Festival, for they also had been there* (John 4:43-45).

Where there is no value; there is elimination of interest, motivation, inspiration, passion, attraction, responsiveness, lack of attention, compassion and there is disorderliness.

Chapter Seven
JESUS' PRIMARY OBJECTIVES

What are Jesus' primary objectives? Jesus' primary objectives were to promote God and the values of the Lord. This he demonstrated severally:

a. When he was called good master and he said, 'Only God that is good.'
b. When he was called master, he told them 'I am not the master but God is.'
c. When they called him teacher and he said to them, 'God is the teacher.'

Jesus answered, "I am the way and the truth and the life. No one comes to the Father except through me" (John 14:6).

After Jesus said this, he looked toward heaven and prayed: "Father, the hour has come. Glorify your Son, that your Son may glorify you. For you granted him authority over all people that he might give eternal life to all those you have given him. Now this is eternal life: that they know you, the only true God, and Jesus Christ, whom you have sent. I have brought you glory on earth by finishing the work you gave me to do. And now, Father, glorify me in your presence with the glory I had with you before the world began.' I have revealed you to those whom you gave me out of the world. They were yours; you gave them to me and they have obeyed your word. Now they know that everything you have given me comes from you. For I gave them the words you gave me and they accepted them. They knew with certainty that I came from you, and they believed that you sent me. I pray for them. I am not praying for the world, but for those you have given me, for they are yours. All I have is yours, and all you have is mine. And glory has come to me through them. I will remain in the world no longer, but they are still in the world, and I am coming to you. Holy Father, protect them by the power of your name, the name you gave me, so that they may be one as we are one. While I was with them, I protected them and kept them safe by that name you gave me. None has been lost except the one doomed to destruction so that Scripture would be fulfilled. I am coming to you now, but I say these things while I am still in the world, so that they may have the full measure of my joy within them. I have given them your word and the world has hated them, for they are not of the world any more than I am of the world. My prayer is not that you take them out of the world but that you protect them from the evil one. They are not of the world, even as I am not of it. Sanctify them by the truth; your word is truth. As you sent me into the world, I have sent them into the world. For them I sanctify myself, that they too may be truly sanctified. My prayer is not for them alone. I pray also for those who will believe in me through their message, that all of them may be one, Father, just as you are in me and I am in you. May they also be in us so that the world may believe that you have sent me? I have given them the glory that you gave me, that they may be one as we are one— I in them and you in me—so that they may be brought to complete unity. Then the world will know that you sent me and have loved them even as you have loved me. Father, I want those you have given me to be with me where I am, and to see my glory, the glory you have given me because you loved me before the creation of the world. Righteous Father, though the world does not know you, I know you, and they know that you have sent me. I have made you known to them, and will continue to make you known in order that the love you have for me may be in them and that I myself may be in them" (John 17:1-26).'

Jesus was also promoting the oneness of value with the father. It is interesting to let you know even the Holy Spirit is commissioned to promote the value of God, the head as well as that of the son. He has no personal word but the words he speaks to us are directly from the father. It is very shocking today, how many preachers are promoting their personal values, ministries, church and their gifts, hence neglecting their commissioner. It is sad news indeed! The gifts Christ gave to men were not to promote their selfish values, or to build ungodly influences, popularity, wealth, riches, settlement, chains of cars, houses and personal empire. But, the actual purpose of the gifts is to promote the Lord's value and to build the saints.

But to each one of us grace has been given as Christ apportioned it. This is why it says: "When he ascended on high, he took many captives and gave gifts to his people." (What does "he ascended" mean except that he also descended to the lower, earthly regions?

He who descended is the very one who ascended higher than all the heavens, in order to fill the whole universe). So Christ himself gave the apostles, the prophets, the evangelists, the pastors and teachers, to equip his people for works of service, so that the body of Christ may be built up until we all reach unity in the faith and in the knowledge of the Son of God and become mature, attaining to the whole measure of the fullness of Christ. Then we will no longer be infants, tossed back and forth by the waves, and blown here and there by every wind of teaching and by the cunning and craftiness of people in their deceitful scheming. Instead, speaking the truth in love, we will grow to become in every respect the mature body of him who is the head, that is, Christ. From him the whole body, joined and held together by every supporting ligament, grows and builds itself up in love, as each part does its work (Ephesians 4:7-15).

Now about the gifts of the Spirit, brothers and sisters, I do not want you to be uninformed. You know that when you were pagans, somehow or other you were influenced and led astray to mute idols. Therefore I want you to know that no one who is speaking by the Spirit of God says, "Jesus be cursed," and no one can say, "Jesus is Lord," except by the Holy Spirit. There are different kinds of gifts, but the same Spirit distributes them. There are different kinds of service, but the same Lord. There are different kinds of working, but in all of them and in everyone it is the same God at work. Now to each one the manifestation of the Spirit is given for the common good. To one there is given through the Spirit a message of wisdom, to another a message of knowledge by means of the same Spirit, to another faith by the same Spirit, to another gifts of healing by that one Spirit, to another miraculous powers, to another prophecy, to another distinguishing between spirits, to another speaking in different kinds of tongues, and to still another the interpretation of tongues. All these are the work of one and the same Spirit, and he distributes them to each one, just as he determines. Just as a body, though one has many parts, but all its many parts form one body, so it is with Christ. For we were all baptized by one Spirit so as to form one body—whether Jews or Gentiles, slave or free—and we were all given the one Spirit to drink (1Corinthians 12:1-13).

For just as each of us has one body with many members, and these members do not all have the same function, so in Christ we, though many, form one body, and each member belongs to all the others. We have different gifts, according to the grace given to each of us. If your gift is prophesying, then prophesy in accordance with your faith; if it is serving, then serve; if it is teaching, then teach; if it is to encourage, then give encouragement; if it is giving, then give generously; if it is to lead, do it diligently; if it is to show mercy, do it cheerfully. Love must be sincere. Hate what is evil; cling to what is good. Be devoted to one another in love. Honour one another above yourselves. Never be lacking in zeal, but keep your spiritual fervour, serving the Lord. Be joyful in hope, patient in affliction, and faithful in prayer. Share with the Lord's people who are in need. Practice hospitality. Bless those who persecute you; bless and do not curse. Rejoice with those who rejoice; mourn with those who mourn. Live in harmony with one another. Do not be proud, but be willing to associate with people of low position. Do not be conceited. Do not repay anyone evil for evil. Be careful to do what is right in the eyes of everyone. If it is possible, as far as it depends on you, live at peace with everyone. Do not take revenge, my dear friends, but leave room for God's wrath, for it is written: "It is mine to avenge; I will repay," says the Lord. On the contrary: "If your enemy is hungry, feed him; if he is thirsty, give him something to drink. In doing this, you will heap burning coals on his head." Do not be overcome by evil, but overcome evil with good (Romans 12:4-21).

All gifts are directly from God. His primary, holy purpose is to promote value of His kingdom against promoting ourselves and directing people's attention towards us.

But mark this: There will be terrible times in the last days. People will be lovers of themselves, lovers of money, boastful, proud, abusive, disobedient to their parents, ungrateful, unholy, without love, unforgiving, slanderous, without self-control, brutal, not lovers of the good, treacherous, rash, conceited, lovers of pleasure rather than lovers of God—having a form of godliness but denying its power. Have nothing to do with such people. They are the kind who worm their way into homes and gain control over gullible women, who are loaded down with sins and are swayed by all kinds of evil desires, always learning but never able to come to a knowledge of the truth. Just as Jannes and Jambres opposed Moses, so also these teachers oppose the truth. They are men of depraved minds, who, as far as the faith is concerned, are rejected. But they will not get very far because, as in the case of those men, their folly will be clear to everyone. You, however, know all about my teaching, my way of life, my purpose, faith, patience, love, endurance, persecutions, sufferings—what kinds of things happened to me in Antioch, Iconium and Lystra, the persecutions I endured. Yet the Lord rescued me from all of them. In fact, everyone who wants to live a godly life in Christ Jesus will be persecuted, while evildoers and impostors will go from bad to worse, deceiving and being deceived. But as for you, continue in what you have learned and have become convinced of, because you know those from whom you learned it, and how from infancy you have known the Holy Scriptures, which are able to make you wise for salvation through faith in Christ Jesus. All Scripture is God-breathed and is useful for teaching, rebuking, correcting and training in righteousness, so that the servant of God may be thoroughly equipped for every good work (2 Timothy 3:1-17).

The Spirit clearly says that in later times some will abandon the faith and follow deceiving spirits and things taught by demons (1Timothy 4:1).

This is spirit of sedition, diversion, deviation and distraction. That is why some men of God are becoming more popular than their God. Unbelievers are willing to accept great men of God and give millions of money to them; and not accept their God. What a shame and disgrace. There is great need to aggressively and forcefully promote God's values. God is tired of all this nonsense. Marketing ourselves through God is great sin; we must repent because God is coming with great judgment.

Let the one who does wrong continue to do wrong; let the vile person continue to be vile; let the one who does right continue to do right; and let the holy person continue to be holy (Revelation 22:11).

Parable of the Wicked Vine Dresser

"Listen to another parable: There was a landowner who planted a vineyard. He put a wall around it, dug a wine press in it and built a watchtower. Then he rented the vineyard to some farmers and moved to another place. When the harvest time approached, he sent his servants to the tenants to collect his fruit. The tenants seized his servants; they beat one, killed another, and stoned a third. Then he sent other servants to them, more than the first time, and the tenants treated them the same way. Last of all, he sent his son to them. 'They will respect my son,' he said. But when the tenants saw the son, they said to each other, 'This is the heir. Come, let's kill him and take his inheritance.' So they took him and threw him out of the vineyard and killed him. Therefore, when the owner of the vineyard comes, what will he do to those tenants?"
'He will bring those wretches to a wretched end,' they replied, 'and he will rent the vineyard to other tenants, who will give him his share of the crop at harvest time.' Jesus said to them, 'Have you never read in the Scriptures: 'the stone the builders rejected

has become the cornerstone; the Lord has done this, and it is marvelous in our eyes?' Therefore I tell you that the kingdom of God will be taken away from you and given to a people who will produce its fruit. Anyone who falls on this stone will be broken to pieces; anyone on whom it falls will be crushed. When the chief priests and the Pharisees heard Jesus' parables, they knew he was talking about them. They looked for a way to arrest him, but they were afraid of the crowd because the people held that he was a prophet (Matthew 21:33-46).

The vine dresser did not value the owner of the vineyard; people who do not value your authority cannot be accountable or submissive, and cannot be loyal. They are planted to cause you annoyance and make you angry. Lack of value can initiate wicked plots. This was the same story about Joseph; his brothers did not value the anointing upon him. They hated Joseph and intended to kill him. God delivered, favoured and made him a Prime Minister in Egypt.

Joseph's story changed from demotion to promotion. God will promote you; it might seem hard and tough today, but tomorrow your story will change if you preserve and protect your primary value which is your focus on God. *And without faith it is impossible to please God, because anyone who comes to him must believe that he exists and that he rewards those who earnestly seek him* (Hebrews 11:6). *But seek first his kingdom and his righteousness, and all these things will be given to you as well* (Matthew 6:33).

Let us look at the story of the vine dresser. If they had valued the land owners, they would not have killed his servants and son. Where there is absence of value, anything evil can happen.

Listen to another parable: There was a landowner who planted a vineyard. He put a wall around it, dug a wine press in it and built a watchtower. Then he rented the vineyard to some farmers and moved to another place. When the harvest time approached, he sent his servants to the tenants to collect his fruit. The tenants seized his servants; they beat one, killed another, and stoned a third. Then he sent other servants to them, more than the first time, and the tenants treated them the same way. Last of all, he sent his son to them. 'They will respect my son,' he said. But when the tenants saw the son, they said to each other, 'This is the heir. Come, let's kill him and take his inheritance.' So they took him and threw him out of the vineyard and killed him. Therefore, when the owner of the vineyard comes, what will he do to those tenants? 'He will bring those wretches to a wretched end,' they replied, 'and he will rent the vineyard to other tenants, who will give him his share of the crop at harvest time.' Jesus said to them, 'Have you never read in the Scriptures: 'the stone the builders rejected has become the cornerstone the Lord has done this, and it is marvellous in our eyes?' Therefore I tell you that the kingdom of God will be taken away from you and given to a people who will produce its fruit. Anyone who falls on this stone will be broken to pieces; anyone on whom it falls will be crushed. When the chief priests and the Pharisees heard Jesus' parables, they knew he was talking about them. They looked for a way to arrest him, but they were afraid of the crowd because the people held that he was a prophet (Matthew 21:33-46).

It is interesting to note that every employer employs people to promote their value and not people that will kill the value of their organisation. But people, who will respect, promote, protect and honour their values.

Jesus spoke to them again in parables, saying: "The kingdom of heaven is like a king who prepared a wedding banquet for his son. He sent his servants to those who had been invited to the banquet to tell them to come, but they refused to come. Then he sent some more servants and said, 'tell those who have been invited that I have prepared my dinner: My oxen and fattened cattle have been butchered, and everything is ready. Come to the wedding banquet.' But they paid no attention and went off—one to his field, another to his business. The rest seized his servants, mistreated them and killed them. The king was enraged. He sent his army and destroyed those murderers and burned their city. Then he said to his servants, 'The wedding banquet is ready, but those I invited did not deserve to come. So go to the street corners and invite to the banquet anyone you find.' So the servants went out into the streets and gathered all the people they could find, the bad as well as the good, and the wedding hall was filled with guests. But when the king came in to see the guests, he noticed a man there who was not wearing wedding clothes. He asked, 'How did you get in here without wedding clothes, friend?' The man was speechless. Then the king told the attendants, 'Tie him hand

and foot, and throw him outside, into the darkness, where there will be weeping and gnashing of teeth.' For many are invited, but few are chosen (Matthew 22:1-14).

The Parable of the Sower

The parable of the sower talks about values and absence of values. If you notice, it was the seed that fell on good soil that brought forth thirty, sixty and one-hundred fold. Those that received the word of God placed value on it, protected, respected and honoured. It is only what you value that works, what you refuse to value never works and that is why it did not work for the one that fell on the roadside, on thorns and on rocks.

That same day Jesus went out of the house and sat by the lake. Such large crowds gathered around him that he got into a boat and sat in it, while all the people stood on the shore. Then he told them many things in parables, saying: 'A farmer went out to sow his seed. As he was scattering the seed, some fell along the path, and the birds came and ate it up. Some fell on rocky places, where it did not have much soil. It sprang up quickly, because the soil was shallow. But when the sun came up, the plants were scorched, and they withered because they had no root. Other seed fell among thorns, which grew up and choked the plants. Still other seed fell on good soil, where it produced a crop—a hundred, sixty or thirty times what was sown. Whoever has ears, let them hear?'

The disciples came to him and asked, 'Why do you speak to the people in parables?' He replied, 'Because the knowledge of the secrets of the kingdom of heaven has been given to you, but not to them. Whoever has will be given more, and they will have abundance. Whoever does not have, even what they have will be taken from them. This is why I speak to them in parables: "Though seeing, they do not see; though hearing, they do not hear or understand. In them is fulfilled the prophecy of Isaiah: 'You will be ever hearing but never understanding; you will be ever seeing but never perceiving. For this people's heart has become calloused; they hardly hear with their ears, and they have closed their eyes. Otherwise they might see with their eyes, hear with their ears, understand with their hearts and turn, and I would heal them." But blessed are your eyes because they see, and your ears because they hear. For truly I tell you, many prophets and righteous people longed to see what you see but did not see it, and to hear what you hear but did not hear it. "Listen then to what the parable of the sower means: When anyone hears the message about the kingdom and does not understand it, the evil one comes and snatches away what was sown in their heart. This is the seed sown along the path. The seed falling on rocky ground refers to someone who hears the word and at once receives it with joy. But since they have no root, they last only a short time. When trouble or persecution comes because of the word, they quickly fall away. The seed falling among the thorns refers to someone who hears the word, but the worries of this life and the deceitfulness of wealth choke the word, making it unfruitful. But the seed falling on good soil refers to someone who hears the word and understands it.

This is the one who produces a crop, yielding a hundred, sixty or thirty times what was sown' (Matthew 13:1-23).

The Parable of the Wheat and Tares

Jesus told them another parable: "The kingdom of heaven is like a man who sowed good seed in his field. But while everyone was sleeping, his enemy came and sowed weeds among the wheat, and went away. When the wheat sprouted and formed heads, then the weeds also appeared. The owner's servants came to him and said, 'Sir, didn't you sow good seed in your field? Where then did the weeds come from?' 'An enemy did this,' he replied. The servants asked him, 'Do you want us to go and pull them up?' 'No,' he answered, 'because while you are pulling the weeds, you may uproot the wheat with them. Let both grow together until the harvest. At that time I will tell the harvesters: First collect the weeds and tie them in bundles to be burned; then gather the wheat and bring it into my barn'" (Matthew 13:24-30).'

Then he left the crowd and went into the house. His disciples came to him and said, 'Explain to us the parable of the weeds in the field.' He answered, 'The one who sowed the good seed is the Son of Man. The field is the world, and the good seed stands for the people of the kingdom. The weeds are the people of the evil one, and the enemy who sows them is the devil. The harvest is the end of the age, and the harvesters are angels. As the weeds are pulled up and burned in the fire, so it will be at the end of the age. The Son of Man will send out his angels, and they will weed out of his kingdom everything that causes sin and all who do evil. They will throw them into the blazing furnace, where there will be weeping and gnashing of teeth. Then the righteous will shine like the sun in the kingdom of their Father. Whoever has ears, let them hear' (Matthew 13:36-43).

The aim of every thief is to kill, destroy and steal.

The thief comes only to steal and kill and destroy; I have come that they may have life, and have it to the full (John 10:10).

The enemy will always want to carry bad news, not good news. His objectives are to demote people, destroy their image, steal their reputation and kill their dreams. Anything that is good, the enemy wants to spoil and defile, to reduce to nothing and to render of no value. There are lots of believers who have talents in our churches; but there could also be great gossips and slanderers the devil plants to destroy their value. Ungodly competition, hatred, jealousy, envy and wickedness can also reduce the value of gifts in the body of Christ. We are not commissioned to tear down one another in the body of Christ but rather to promote the values of God and that of His kingdom.

Now about the gifts of the Spirit, brothers and sisters, I do not want you to be uninformed. You know that when you were pagans, somehow or other you were influenced and led astray to mute idols. Therefore I want you to know that no one who is speaking by the Spirit of God says, "Jesus be cursed," and no one can say, "Jesus is Lord," except by the Holy Spirit. There are different kinds of gifts, but the same Spirit distributes them. There are different kinds of service, but the same Lord. There are different kinds of working, but in all of them and in everyone it is the same God at work. Now to each one the manifestation of the Spirit is given for the common good. To one there is given through the Spirit a message of wisdom, to another a message of knowledge by means of the same Spirit, to another faith by the same Spirit, to another gifts of healing by that one Spirit, to another miraculous powers, to another prophecy, to another distinguishing between spirits, to another speaking in different kinds of tongues, and to still another the interpretation of tongues. All these are the work of one and the same Spirit, and he distributes them to each one, just as he determines. Just as a body, though one, has many parts, but all its many parts form one body, so it is with Christ. For we were all baptized by one Spirit so as to form one body—whether Jews or Gentiles, slave or free—and we were all given the one Spirit to drink. Even so the body is not made up of one part but of many. Now if the foot should say, "Because I am not a hand, I do not belong to the body," it would not for that reason stop being part of the body. And if the ear should say, "Because I am not an eye, I do not belong to the body," it would not for that reason stop being part of the body. If the whole body were an eye, where would the sense of hearing be? If the whole body were an ear, where would the sense of smell be? But in fact God has placed the parts in the body, every one of them, just as he wanted them to be. If they were all one part, where would the body be? As it is, there are many parts, but one body. The eye cannot say to the hand, "I don't need you!" And the head cannot say to the feet, "I don't need you!" On the contrary, those parts of the body that seem to be weaker are indispensable, and the parts that we think are less honourable we treat with special honour. And the parts that are not presentable are treated with special modesty, while our presentable parts need no special treatment. But God has put the body together, giving greater honour to the parts that lacked it, so that there should be no division in the body, but that its parts should have equal concern for each other. If one part suffers, every part suffers with it; if one part is honoured, every part rejoices with it. Now you are the body of Christ, and each one of you is a part of it. And God has placed in the church first of all apostles, second prophets, third teachers, then miracles, then gifts of healing, of helping, of guidance, and of different kinds of tongues. Are all apostles? Are all prophets? Are all teachers? Do all work miracles? Do all have gifts of healing? Do all speak in tongues? Do all interpret? Now eagerly desire the greater gifts (1 Corinthians 12:1-31).

Perilous Anointing

Initiates promoting self instead of God. The Spirit clearly says that in later times some will abandon the faith and follow deceiving spirits and things taught by demons. Such teachings come through hypocritical liars, whose consciences have been seared as with a hot iron. They forbid people to marry and order them to abstain from certain foods, which God created to be received with thanksgiving by those who believe and who know the truth. For everything God created is good, and nothing is to be rejected if it is received with thanksgiving, because it is consecrated by the word of God and prayer. If you point these things out to the brothers and sisters, you will be a good minister of Christ Jesus, nourished on the truths of the faith and of the good teaching that you have followed. Have nothing to do with godless myths and old wives' tales; rather, train yourself to be godly. For physical training is of some value, but godliness has value for all things, holding promise for both the present life and the life to come. This is a trustworthy saying that deserves full acceptance. That is why we labour and strive, because we have put our hope in the living God, who is the Saviour of all people, and especially of those who believe. Command and teach these things. Don't let anyone look down on you because you are young, but set an example for the believers in speech, in conduct, in love, in faith and in purity. Until I come, devote yourself to the public reading of Scripture, to preaching and to teaching. Do not neglect your gift, which was given you through prophecy when the body of elders laid their hands on you. Be diligent in these matters; give yourself wholly to them, so that everyone may see your progress. Watch your life and doctrine closely. Persevere in them, because if you do, you will save both yourself and your hearers (1Timothy 4).

But mark this: There will be terrible times in the last days. People will be lovers of themselves, lovers of money, boastful, proud, abusive, disobedient to their parents, ungrateful, unholy, without love, unforgiving, slanderous, without self-control, brutal, not lovers of the good, treacherous, rash, conceited, lovers of pleasure rather than lovers of God— having a form of godliness but denying its power. Have nothing to do with such people. They are the kind who worm their way into homes and gain control over gullible women, who are loaded down with sins and are swayed by all kinds of evil desires, always learning but never able to come to a knowledge of the truth. Just as Jannes and Jambres opposed Moses, so also these teachers oppose the truth. They are men of depraved minds, who, as far as the faith is concerned, are rejected. But they will not get very far because, as in the case of those men, their folly will be clear to everyone. You, however, know all about my teaching, my way of life, my purpose, faith, patience, love, endurance, persecutions, sufferings—what kinds of things happened to me in Antioch, Iconium and Lystra, the persecutions I endured. Yet the Lord rescued me from all of them. In fact, everyone who wants to live a godly life in Christ Jesus will be persecuted, while evildoers and impostors will go from bad to worse, deceiving and being deceived. But as for you, continue in what you have learned and have become convinced of, because you know those from whom you learned it, and how from infancy you have known the Holy scriptures, which are able to make you wise for salvation through faith in Christ Jesus. All scripture is God-breathed and is useful for teaching, rebuking, correcting and training in righteousness, so that the servant of God may be thoroughly equipped for every good work (2 Timothy 3).

The spirit of anti-Christ causes:

1. Self-promotion
2. Self-announcement
3. Self-advertisement

We are called to promote the values of God and those of his Kingdom.

∼

Chapter Eight
GOD'S CONCEPT OF VALUE

God works with value. God does not appear in places where He is not valued and respected. God valued His church which established and made decree to protect her value.

When Jesus came to the region of Caesarea Philippi, he asked his disciples, "Who do people say the Son of Man is?" They replied, "Some say John the Baptist; others say Elijah; and still others, Jeremiah or one of the prophets." "But what about you?" he asked. "Who do you say I am?" Simon Peter answered, "You are the Messiah, the Son of the living God." Jesus replied, "Blessed are you, Simon son of Jonah, for this was not revealed to you by flesh and blood, but by my Father in heaven. And I tell you that you are Peter, and on this rock I will build my church, and the gates of Hades will not overcome it. I will give you the keys of the kingdom of heaven; whatever you bind on earth will be bound in heaven, and whatever you loose on earth will be loosed in heaven (Matthew 16:13-19).

God blacklisted and put into watch list certain negative behaviour and action that does not promote values of God and His church. God is all knowing, and knew the danger of forsaking and neglecting values. Killing value is same as killing life.

A troublemaker and a villain, who goes about with a corrupt mouth, who winks maliciously with his eye, signals with his feet and motions with his fingers, who plots evil with deceit in his heart he always stirs up conflict Therefore disaster will overtake him in an instant; he will suddenly be destroyed—without remedy. There are six things the Lord hates, seven that are detestable to him: haughty eyes, a lying tongue, hands that shed innocent blood, a heart that devises wicked schemes, feet that are quick to rush into evil, a false witness who pours out lies and a person who stirs up conflict in the community (Proverbs 6:12-19).

But they mocked God's messengers, despised his words and scoffed at his prophets until the wrath of the Lord was aroused against his people and there was no remedy (2 Chronicles 36:16).

Are not the cords of their tent pulled up, so that they die without wisdom?' (Job 4:21).

He says to himself, "God will never notice; he covers his face and never sees." (Psalm 10:11).

Cain and Abel Concept

When Cain killed Abel, he killed value. Abel's value was killed; his growth, vision, assignment for God and his generation was put to an end. Cain killing his brother Abel was neglect of value and recognition of value. Life is about value. Value helps to protect and preserve life. It helps to restrain people from doing harm to themselves and to others.

The thief comes only to steal and kill and destroy; I have come that they may have life, and have it to the full (John 10:10).

A thief does not kill, steal, and destroy until value is neglected. Jesus commissioned us to life abundance. It is centered on placement of value. Jesus laying down his life for us was centered on value. He suffering death, resurrection, ascension and coming back is fundamentally centered on value. God giving his only son to rescue us was based on value.

For God so loved the world that he gave his one and only Son, that whoever believes in him shall not perish but have eternal life (John 3:16).

Daniel refusing to pray to God of Darius except living God is centered on value. Joseph refusing to sleep with his master wife was based on values, value for God, value for his master and value for his dream.

It pleased Darius to appoint 120 satraps to rule throughout the kingdom, with three administrators over them, one of whom was Daniel. The satraps were made accountable to them so that the king might not suffer loss. Now Daniel so distinguished himself among the administrators and the satraps by his exceptional qualities that the king planned to set him over the whole kingdom.

At this, the administrators and the satraps tried to find grounds for charges against Daniel in his conduct of government affairs, but they were unable to do so. They could find no corruption in him, because he was trustworthy and neither corrupt nor negligent. Finally these men said, "We will never find any basis for charges against this man Daniel unless it has something to do with the law of his God."

So these administrators and satraps went as a group to the king and said: "May King Darius live forever! The royal administrators, prefects, satraps, advisers and governors have all agreed that the king should issue an edict and enforce the decree that anyone who prays to any god or human being during the next thirty days, except to you, Your Majesty, shall be thrown into the lions' den. Now, Your Majesty, issue the decree and put it in writing so that it cannot be altered—in accordance with the law of the Medes and Persians, which cannot be repealed." So King Darius put the decree in writing. Now when Daniel learned that the decree had been published, he went home to his upstairs room where the windows opened toward Jerusalem. Three times a day he got down on his knees and prayed, giving thanks to his God, just as he had done before. Then these men went as a group and found Daniel praying and asking God for help. So they went to the king and spoke to him about his royal decree: "Did you not publish a decree that during the next thirty days anyone who prays to any god or human being except to you, Your Majesty, would be thrown into the lions' den?" The king answered, "The decree stands—in accordance with the law of the Medes and

Persians, which cannot be repealed." Then they said to the king, "Daniel, who is one of the exiles from Judah, pays no attention to you, Your Majesty, or to the decree you put in writing. He still prays three times a day." When the king heard this, he was greatly distressed; he was determined to rescue Daniel and made every effort until sundown to save him. Then the men went as a group to King Darius and said to him, "Remember, Your Majesty, that according to the law of the Medes and Persians no decree or edict that the king issues can be changed." So the king gave the order, and they brought Daniel and threw him into the lions' den. The king said to Daniel, "May your God, whom you serve continually, rescue you!" A stone was brought and placed over the mouth of the den, and the king sealed it with his own signet ring and with the rings of his nobles, so that Daniel's situation might not be changed. Then the king returned to his palace and spent the night without eating and without any entertainment being brought to him. And he could not sleep. At the first light of dawn, the king got up and hurried to the lions' den. When he came near the den, he called to Daniel in an anguished voice, "Daniel, servant of the living God, has your God, whom you serve continually, been able to rescue you from the lions?" Daniel answered, "May the king live forever! My God sent his angel, and he shut the mouths of the lions. They have not hurt me, because I was found innocent in his sight. Nor have I ever done any wrong before you, Your Majesty." The king was overjoyed and gave orders to lift Daniel out of the den. And when Daniel was lifted from the den, no wound was found on him, because he had trusted in his God. At the king's command, the men who had falsely accused Daniel were *brought in and thrown into the lions' den, along with their wives and children. And before they reached the floor of the den, the lions overpowered them and crushed all their bones. Then King Darius wrote to all the nations and peoples of every language in all the earth: "May you prosper greatly! "I issue a decree that in every part of my kingdom people must fear and reverence the God of Daniel. "For he is the living God and he endures forever; his kingdom will not be destroyed, his dominion will never end. He rescues and he saves; he performs signs and wonders in the heavens and on the earth. He has rescued Daniel. From the power of the lions." So Daniel prospered during the reign of Darius and the reign of Cyrus the Persian* (Daniel 6:1-28).

Case Studies of 'Familiarity' Characters in the Bible

Familiarity has an attitude of reducing the weight of authority and water down value; it can cause blockages of receiving from God and man, because what you don't value doesn't work for you. Familiarity has an enabling power to disregard power; this can be seen in the following case studies of various characters in the bible.

Lucifer: *How you have fallen from heaven, morning star, son of the dawn! You have been cast down to the earth, you who once laid low the nations! You said in your heart, "I will ascend to the heavens; I will raise my throne above the stars of God; I will sit enthroned on the mount of assembly, on the utmost heights of Mount Zaphon. I will ascend above the tops of the clouds; I will* *make myself like the Most High." But you are brought down to the realm of the dead, to the depths of the pit, those who see you stare at you, they ponder your fate: "Is this the man who shook the earth and made kingdoms tremble"* (Isaiah 14:12-16).

This 'familiarity' spirit is Lucifer, when he was leading praises in heaven. He was so familiar with God that he wanted to be God. God threw him out of Heaven. Familiarity not properly handled is capable of inciting rebellion, disobedience, disloyalty and insult. This situation called familiarity should not be taken lightly. If your situation reflects this circumstance, no matter how familiar you are with your boss, retain their value and give them due respect. This will secure a long-term relationship and reward. It is better to be retained than to be cast away.

Cain and God: This was a dangerous situation of creature arguing with his creator. Cain played spirit of familiarity when God asked about his brother and his reply was 'am I my brother's keeper?' That was an attitude of familiarity spirit, which initiates lack of duty and care.

Miriam, Aaron and Moses: Moses was said to be the meekest man on earth, which made him accessible to congregation of Israel. Miriam and Aaron were abused by demanding the 'only Prophet in camp', which resulted in curse to Miriam and degradation to Aaron. They had to repent for God to heal Miriam. Things will remain the same in church unless there is genuine repentance.

Elisha and His Servant: This servant was familiar with Elisha; he lost spiritual touch in continually remembering that Elisha was a Prophet of God. You have to continually remind ourselves of value system or else holy things may mean little or have no meaning to your life and your ministry.

∼

Chapter Nine
VALUE & ACCOUNTABILITY

Value and accountability are keys to greatness. It is the oil of promotion and advancement. To be accountable qualifies you for employability but lack of accountability is disqualification. Employers cannot hire someone that is unaccountable or not submissive. It is disgraceful, immature and ignorant to deny your employer or your line manager submission or accountability. Where accountability is absent, there will be confusion, division and destruction.

The following are characteristics of an unaccountable person and negative effects to organisation, family, church and any other institution.

1.   Where there is absence of accountability, there is lack of submission. It is a dangerous sign of disaster.

2.   Absence of accountability is sign of pride, arrogance and self-centredness. This is oil from pit of hell. This kind of person does not represent God's values; lacks light and dwells in darkness. Trinity does not produce bad behaviour; they behave well and work in coordinated divine order. They are commissioned and commissioners of unity. Where God dwells, the flesh has no say. The spirit has a sound mind but devil does not, therefore we should put flesh to

death. It is flesh that manipulates mankind into dangerous behaviour.

Very truly I tell you, unless a kernel of wheat falls to the ground and dies, it remains only a single seed. But if it dies, it produces many seeds (John 12:24).

3.Lack of accountability initiates division, disorder and confusion. This attitude is not of God. God is not an author of confusion.

4.Where there is absence of accountability, it initiates administrative errors, complication and organisational failure. It is like a car without brakes. What will happen? It will head towards disaster.

5.Where there is no accountability, it is a sign of disobedience. Disobedience is disconnection from organisation. For example: employee from employer, believer and God, children and parents etc.

6.Absence of accountability is a sign of stubbornness, rudeness and high mindedness. This is near witchcraft. It is actually witchcraft; witches and wizards do not and cannot be accountable to light except by compulsion. They are disobedient and stubborn agents of darkness.

7.	Where there is no accountability, there is absence of value and recognition of organisation and leadership; it encourages devaluation. Where there is no value, there will be insult and dishonour.

8.	Where there is no accountability, it breeds disrespect, dishonour and disregard to organisational working principle, value and leadership. An employee that does not respect his employer has disempowered the employer. If the situation is not taken care of, the employer's words become noise and this might destroy teamwork. Then comes leadership failure and interrupts chain of leadership. The work of poison is to kill; dishonour is like poison, whether directly or indirectly. It is action, behaviour, expression, reaction, communication, absence, response and disregard.

Although you have been forsaken and hated, with no one travelling through, I will make you the everlasting pride and the joy of all generations (Isaiah 60:15).

Instead of your shame you will receive a double portion, and instead of disgrace you will rejoice in your inheritance. And so you will inherit a double portion in your land, and everlasting joy will be yours (Isaiah 61:7).

9.	Lack of accountability initiates instability in organisations. A person that refuses to be accountable is a problem creator. We were not born to create problems but solutions. Eliminate the problem and implement solution.

10. Lack of accountability, initiates communication blockage and therefore results in conflicts. If important information for development of an organisation is withheld, there will be a negative impact on organisation. This is another satanic behaviour.

11. Lack of accountability is not good testimony for any believer and also bad character reference.

12. Lack of accountability causes structural damage and disorganisation. An unaccountable person is an agent of disorganisation. It is a thief and adversary.

The thief comes only to steal and kill and destroy; I have come that they may have life, and have it to the full (John 10:10).

13. Absence of accountability breeds suspicion, misunderstanding, assumption, omission, probability of errors, and uncertainty of things, empty imagination and annoyance. When there is accountability and information, there is empowerment to overcome all forms of assumptions. This helps ascertain there is no hidden agenda.

14. Where there is no accountability, there is corruption. A place of corruption is a place of confusion.

15. A person who refuses to be accountable has dismissed the superior's authority and ability to lead. It is creative

intention to remove your crown of leadership. This was the picture of Satan to God.

How you have fallen from heaven, morning star, son of the dawn! You have been cast down to the earth, you who once laid low the nations! You said in your heart, "I will ascend to the heavens; I will raise my throne above the stars of God; I will sit enthroned on the mount of assembly, on the utmost heights of Mount Zaphon. I will ascend above the tops of the clouds; I will make myself like the Most High." But you are brought down to the realm of the dead, to the depths of the pit. Those who see you stare at you, they ponder your fate: "Is this the man who shook the earth and made kingdoms tremble, the man who made the world a wilderness, who overthrew its cities and would not let his captives go home?" (Isaiah 14:12-17)

16.   Lack of accountability causes a breakdown of communication and death of relationship. A person who is not accountable to you is not with you.

17.   Lack of accountability is a sign of bad report and bad reference. It does not guarantee a job. It is disempowering and disablement in nature.

18.   Lack of accountability is corruption. Where there is no openness, there is an organisational problem. Where such problems exists, development is hindered. Achievement is made below expectation. It is not known whether personnel are working hard to fulfil and meet target.

19.   Lack of accountability is lack of fear of God and man. This attitude proceeds from self-centredness. It is Lucifer's spirit. Satan was rebellious to God. He refused to be submissive and accountable to God in heaven. Pride got into his head. He wanted to be like God. God humbled him and cast him down. There was also a judge who does not fear man or God. That means he is not accountable to God and man. This kind of person cannot be employed in any organisation, if that organisation wants to make progress and advancement. Don't employ or hire a devil. He will not tell you what he is doing.

20.   Accountability creates good atmosphere for working relationships. It sweetens relationships and creates stable and enjoyable atmosphere.

21.   Accountability ensures work in progress and stable advancement.

22.   Accountability initiates confidence between employer and employee. It is the height of trust and honesty.

23.   Accountability gives room for evaluation and better performance.

24.   Accountability helps to create spirit of excellence.

25.   People who are not accountable are organisational killers. Avoid organisational killers. They can be the following:

i. Professional killers: They kill an organisation through professional disobedience and pride.
ii. Spiritual killers: They are so spiritual with their spirituality, they can kill an organisation because of lack of wisdom, understanding, knowledge, practical obedience, teaching ability, availability, faithfulness, insensible spirituality and unreasonable truce breaker. They lack good practice and spy liberty of saints, putting saints under duress of suspicion.
iii. Men and women of unjust spirit.
iv. Satanic agents: People that follow Satan and cooperate with enemies' manifestation.
v. Self-centred men and women.
vi. Ignorant people.
vii. Unteachable men and women.
viii. Unfaithful men and women.
ix. Unavailable believers with absent mentors.
x. Unbroken men who are drunk but not filled.

We are instructed to develop spiritual resources that will enable us to serve God and his people. *Very truly I tell you, unless a kernel of wheat falls to the ground and dies, it remains only a single seed. But if it dies, it produces many seeds* (John 12:24). *Do not get drunk on wine, which leads to debauchery. Instead, be filled with the Spirit, speaking to one another with psalms, hymns, and songs from the Spirit. Sing and make music from your heart to the Lord, always giving thanks to God the Father for everything, in the name of our Lord Jesus Christ. Submit to one another out of reverence for Christ* (Ephesians 5:18-21). *Jesus, full of the Holy Spirit, left the Jordan and was led by the Spirit into the wilderness, where for forty days he was tempted by the devil. He ate nothing during those days, and at the end of them he was hungry. The devil said to him, "If you are the Son of God, tell this stone to become bread." Jesus answered, "It is written: 'Man shall not live on bread alone.' The devil led him up to a high place and showed him in an instant all the kingdoms of the world. And he said to him, "I will give you all their authority and splendour; it has been given to me, and I can give it to anyone I want to. If you worship me, it will all be yours." Jesus answered, "It is written: 'Worship the Lord your God and serve him only.' The devil led him to Jerusalem and had him stand on the highest point of the temple. "If you are the Son of God," he said, "throw yourself down from here. For it is written: 'He will command his angels concerning you to guard you carefully; they will lift you up in their hands, so that you will not strike your foot against a stone.' Jesus answered, "It is said: 'Do not put the Lord your God to the test.' When the devil had finished all this tempting, he left him until an opportune time.*

Jesus Rejected at Nazareth Jesus returned to Galilee in the power of the Spirit, and news about him spread through the whole countryside. He was teaching in their synagogues, and everyone praised him. He went to Nazareth, where he had been brought up, and on the Sabbath day he went into the synagogue, as was his custom. He stood up to read, and the scroll of the prophet Isaiah was handed to him. Unrolling it, he found the place where it is written: "The Spirit of the Lord is on me, because he has anointed me to proclaim good news to the poor. He has sent me to proclaim freedom for the prisoners and recovery of sight for the blind, to set the oppressed free (Luke 4:1-18).

When the day of Pentecost came, they were all together in one place. Suddenly a sound like the blowing of a violent wind came from heaven and filled the whole house where they were sitting. They saw what seemed to be tongues of fire that separated and came to rest on each of them. All of them were filled with the Holy Spirit and began to speak in other tongues as the Spirit enabled them. Now there were staying in Jerusalem God-fearing Jews from every nation under heaven (Acts 2:1-5).

∼

Chapter Ten
VALUE PRAYER POINTS

The following prayer points can be prayed daily until you received victory and deliverance. Use the prayer point according to your needs.

Victory over Hidden Curses

Confession: Christ redeemed us from the curse of the law by becoming a curse for us, for it is written: "Cursed is everyone who is hung on a pole." He redeemed us in order that the blessing given to Abraham might come to the Gentiles through Christ Jesus, so that by faith we might receive the promise of the Spirit (Galatians 3:13-14).

1. I confess all sins that have given enemy legal right to place any curse on me or my household. Repent, ask God for forgiveness and cleaning.
2. I command all curses issued against me and my family, be broken, in the name of Jesus.
3. I command all evil spirits associated with all these curses to leave me and my family now, in the name of Jesus.
4. I break all inherited curses and I command all spirits associated to inherited curses to leave me now, in the name of Jesus.

5. I renounce and break any curse that may be in my parents' families back to ten generations in the name of Jesus.
6. I renounce and break all curses put on my family line and my descendants in the name of Jesus.
7. I break and cancel every curse placed on me and my family out of jealousy in the name of Jesus.
8. I break and cancel every curse issued by satanic ministers in the name of Jesus.
9. I break and cancel every curse of automatic failure working in my family, in the name of Jesus.
10. I renounce and break self-imposed curses in the name of Jesus.
11. I cancel consequences and evil effects of all curses in the name of Jesus.

There is no divination against Jacob, no evil omens against Israel. It will now be said of Jacob and of Israel, 'See what God has done!' (Numbers 23:23)

I have received a command to bless; he has blessed, and I cannot change it (Numbers 23:20).

Victory over Evil Pattern

Confession: Therefore, if anyone is in Christ, the new creation has come: The old has gone, the new is here! (2 Corinthians 5:17)

1. O God, rearrange my life to conform to your will in Jesus' name.
2. Every pattern of darkness in my life, break in the name of Jesus.
3. Every negative inherited pattern in my life, break by fire, in the name of Jesus.
4. Every evil family pattern in my life and family is broken in the name of Jesus.
5. O God, arise and place me in my divine pattern in Jesus' name.
6. Psalms 126:1 says 'when the Lord turned again the captivity of Zion, we were like them that dreamed.'
7. O God, in the name of Jesus, turn again my captivity today.

Victory over Fear

Confession: For God hath not given us the spirit of fear; but of power and of love, and of a sound mind (2 Timothy 1:7).

1. I renounce, bind and cast out the spirit of fear in my life.
2. I command every terror of night that has brought

fear into my life, come out of me and go in Jesus name.
3. Fear of death, I reject you and command you to lose your hold over my life.
4. You fear of failure, I reject you in Jesus' name.
5. All negative doors opened in the past by spirit of fear, be closed now in Jesus' name.
6. I refuse to be intimidated by any demonic nightmare in the name of Jesus.
7. I decree and declare the expectation of ungodly concerning me will be frustrated.
8. I reject every satanic lie that is tempting me to move away from where God has ordained for my blessing.
9. Thank you Lord because I abide and trust in you, I will not be moved. (Psalms 125).
10. I release the fire of God against every satanic activity trying to make me depart from the faith.
11. God, I give you praise because in the middle of my battle you will lift my horn of anointing. (1Samuel 2:10)
12. I boldly declare that those who have gone too far in their attack of my life and commitment to God, be put to shame.
13. I bless you Lord because you will lift up your hand against the enemy.
14. I pray the wicked and persecutors shall stumble.
15. I declare in spite of their attack and effort they will not prevail.

16. I pray the wicked shall not be able to proceed further with their intentions.
17. Every act of wickedness planned against me shall meet with frustration.
18. I decree the provocation of my adversaries would only result in my promotion.
19. I declare and decree that I am out of satanic attack and provocation, God will bring forth a breakthrough for me.
20. Thank God because He will turn your reproach and in spite of your adversaries to your testimony. (Nehemiah 4:4-5).

Victory over the Spirit of Infirmity (Healing)

(These prayer points are designed to prophesy healing into your situation. They will cause you to have what belongs to you by rights; healing and divine health).

But for you who revere my name, the sun of righteousness will rise with healing in its wings. And you will go out and leap like calves released from the stall (Malachi 4:2).

1. Every knee of infirmity in my life, bow, in the name of Jesus
2. I shall see this sickness no more, in the name of Jesus.
3. Let the whirlwind scatter every vessel of infirmity fashioned against my life in Jesus name.

4. Let all death contractors begin to fight themselves, in Jesus name.
5. Let every germ of infirmity in my body die, in the name of Jesus.
6. Every foundation of spirit husband/wife in my family line is disannulled in the name of Jesus.
7. I command every power preventing me as wife from accepting headship of my husband to be destroyed in the name of Jesus.
8. I command all powers preventing me as husband from living as true head to be destroyed in Jesus name.
9. I command every imagination, thought, plan, decision, desire and expectation of divorce or separation against my marriage to be destroyed in the name of Jesus.
10. (Men) Every evil spiritual dowry paid on my behalf or by myself is withdrawn by fire in name of Jesus.
11. (Women) Every evil spiritual dowry paid for me be returned to spirit husband in the name of Jesus.
12. I break my marriage vow, with spirit husband/wife in the name of Jesus.
13. Every evil wedding ring garment, be burnt to ashes in the name of Jesus.

Victory over Barrenness

For this purpose, the son of God was manifested that he might destroy the works of the devil (1 John 3:8).

1. The God who quickens the dead and calls those things that be not as if they were, answer me by fire, in the name of Jesus.
2. I command, fire of God, saturate my womb in Jesus' name.
3. I renounce, break and release myself from every covenant of unprofitable lateness in child-bearing in the name of Jesus.
4. I break and release myself from every curse issued against my child-bearing in Jesus' name.
5. Let all power-attracting attackers to me during my pregnancy be exposed and destroyed in the name of Jesus.
6. I break every curse of miscarriage and premature rebirth in my life in Jesus' name.
7. I bind and cast out every strong man assigned to my womb, reproductive system and marital life in the name of Jesus.
8. You foreign hand laid on my womb, release me in the name of Jesus.
9. I command every spirit rooted in fornication, sexual perversion and masturbation, to come out of my womb by fire, in the mighty name of Jesus.

10. I command all satanic deposits in my womb to be destroyed by fire of the Holy Spirit, in the name of Jesus.
11. I command all satanic deposits in my reproductive organs, be destroyed by the blood of Jesus.

O God, in the name of the Lord Jesus do creative work in my womb and reproductive system.

I thank you father for answered prayers.

Victory for Pregnant Women and Babies in Womb

When Elizabeth heard Mary's greeting, the baby leaped in her womb, and Elizabeth was filled with the Holy Spirit (Luke 1:41). *But when God, who set me apart from my mother's womb and called me by his grace, was pleased* (Galatians 1:15).

Before I formed you in the womb I knew you, before you were born I set you apart; I appointed you as a prophet to the nations. (Jeremiah 1:5)

1. Thank you, Lord, for a wonderful pregnancy and enjoyable pregnancy.
2. Thank you, Lord, for this child shall be great before you and shall do exploits in your name.

3. I decree no sickness or plague will come upon the Baby, in Jesus' name.
4. I decree soundness, health and wholeness into spirit, soul and body of baby, in Jesus' name.
5. I ban this baby from inheriting any evil thing from our family line, in Jesus' name.
6. I speak wholeness, soundness and perfection into hearts, eyes, ears, skin, bones and teeth of baby, in Jesus' name.
7. Let baby be covered with blood of Jesus and surrounded by hedge of divine fire, in the name of Jesus.
8. I disallow baby from having and accepting any form of infirmity, in the name of Jesus.
9. Let respiratory, digestive and circulatory systems of baby be normal, strong and healthy, in the name of Jesus.
10. You baby, hear the word of the Lord; your position must be head down at birth, in the name of Jesus.
11. O Lord, let the child be saved at early age.
12. O Lord, let child be filled with the Holy Spirit even from womb.
13. O Lord, let child be cleansed from every hereditary problems by the blood of Jesus.
14. Father, I speak to my body and to my baby, every part, organ, system to function properly and perfectly, fully developed as you intended from beginning.
15. I declare health, wholeness, soundness in spirit, soul, and body from top of head to bottom of my feet in Jesus mighty name.

Victory and Deliverance for Stubborn Children

I will instruct you and teach you in the way you should go; I will counsel you with my loving eye on you (Psalms 32:8).
What you decide on will be done, and light will shine on your ways (Job 22:28).

For this reason, since the day we heard about you, we have not stopped praying for you. We continually ask God to fill you with the knowledge of his will through all the wisdom and understanding that the Spirit gives, so that you may live a life worthy of the Lord and please him in every way: bearing fruit in every good work, growing in the knowledge of God (Colossians 1:9-10).

For the unbelieving husband has been sanctified through his wife, and the unbelieving wife has been sanctified through her believing husband. Otherwise your children would be unclean, but as it is, they are holy (1 Corinthians 7:14).

You, dear children, are from God and have overcome them, because the one who is in you is greater than the one who is in the world (1 John 4:4).

Devise your strategy, but it will be thwarted; propose your plan, but it will not stand, for God is with us (Isaiah 8:10).

Here am I, and the children the Lord has given me. We are signs and symbols in Israel from the Lord Almighty, who dwells on Mount Zion (Isaiah 8:18).

The Lord will grant that the enemies who rise up against you will be defeated before you. They will come at you from one direction but flee from you in seven (Deuteronomy 28:7).

The God of peace will soon crush Satan under your feet. The grace of our Lord Jesus be with you (Romans 16:20).

1. I bind every spirit, contrary to the Spirit of God preventing me from enjoying my children, in Jesus' name.
2. I bind every spirit blinding their minds from receiving the glorious light of the gospel of our Lord Jesus Christ, in Jesus' name.
3. Let the spirit of stubbornness, pride and disrespect for parents flee from their lives, in Jesus' name.
4. Father God, destroy everything in my children preventing them from doing your will, in Jesus' name.
5. Every curse, evil covenant and all inherited problems passed down to my children are cancelled, in Jesus' name.
6. Mention their names one by one and tell the Lord what you want them to become.
7. Let the association and agreement between my children and enemies be scattered in Jesus' name.

8. My children will not become misdirected arrows, in Jesus' name.
9. I release my children from bondage of any evil domination, in Jesus' name.
10. Let evil influences by demonic friends clear away, in Jesus' name.
11. You (mention name of child), I disassociate you from any conscious or unconscious demonic grouping or involvement, in Jesus' name.
12. In Jesus' name, I receive mandate and now exercise it to release my children from prison of any strongman.
13. Let God arise and all enemies of my home be scattered, in Jesus' name.
14. Every evil influence and activity of strange women on my children is nullified, in Jesus' name.
15. I thank God for answers to my prayers.

Victory over Death

Confession: I shall not die but live and declare the works of the Lord.

1. My covenant with death shall be disannulled and my agreement with held shall not stand in Jesus' name.
2. I bind and cast out every strongman of death and hell in my life, in Jesus' name.
3. I remove my life from every shadow of death in Jesus' name.

4. I break every unprofitable covenant regarding untimely death in my life in Jesus' name.
5. I remove my life from control of hands of any dead person in Jesus' name.
6. I cancel my name from any death register in Jesus' name.
7. Every grave cloth over my life is removed by fire in Jesus' name.
8. I renounce and break every curse of premature death in Jesus' name.
9. I renounce and break every curse of sudden death over my life in Jesus' name.
10. I break my covenant with sudden death in Jesus' name.
11. I break my covenant with grave in my life in Jesus' name.
12. I shall not die but live and declare the works of the Lord.
13. The Lord is my strength and song, and is become my salvation.
14. With long life will He satisfy me and show me His salvation.

Victory over Satanic Dreams

Confessions: And afterward, I will pour out my Spirit on all people. Your sons and daughters will prophesy, your old men will dream dreams, your young men will see visions (Joel 2:28).

1. I claim all good things I have lost as a result of defeat and attacks in my dream, in Jesus' name.
2. I destroy every manipulation in my life through dreams in Jesus' name.
3. I reject all evil satanic load placed on me through dreams in Jesus' name.
4. I command every arrow, gunshot, wound, harassment and opposition in my dreams to be returned to sender, in Jesus' name.
5. I command every spiritual animal: cats, dogs, snakes that fight me in my dream, be chained in Jesus' name.
6. I break and renounce every covenant and initiation through dreams.
7. I lose myself from curses, hexes, spells, bewitchment and evil domination directed against me through dreams, in Jesus' name.
8. I command all past satanic defeats in my dream to be converted to victory in Jesus' name.
9. I command all bondage in my dream to be converted to freedom.
10. I command every satanic design of oppression against me in my dreams and visions, to be destroyed in Jesus' name.
11. I remove my name from register of evil feeders in my dreams by the blood of Jesus.
12. I bind and cast out, you spirit that brings bad dreams to me, in Jesus' name.
13. Lord Jesus, replace all satanic dreams with heavenly visions and divinely inspired dreams.

Victory over Singleness

Therefore God exalted him to the highest place and gave him the name that is above every name, that at the name of Jesus every knee should bow, in heaven and on earth and under the earth (Philippians 2:9-10).

When you were dead in your sins and in the circumcision of your flesh, God made you alive with Christ. He forgave us all our sins (Colossians 2:13).

They triumphed over him by the blood of the Lamb and by the word of their testimony; they did not love their lives so much as to shrink from death (Revelation 12:11).

For no word from God will ever fail (Luke 1:37).

1. Ask God to forgive you of any sin that would hinder answers to your prayers.
2. I will not cooperate with any anti-marriage spells and curses in Jesus' name.
3. I destroy any bewitchment fashioned against my settling down in marriage, in Jesus' name.
4. I command every force magnetising wrong people to me, be paralysed, in Jesus' name.
5. I cancel every covenant of marital failure and late marriage, in Jesus' name.

6. I break my spiritual wedding conducted consciously or unconsciously on my behalf, in Jesus' name.
7. I decree all forces of manipulating, delaying, or hindering my marriage to be completely paralysed in Jesus' name.
8. I command all evil anti-marriage marks be removed, in Jesus' name.
9. Father God, expose all scheme and plans of Satan devised against me through any source at any time, in Jesus' name.
10. I turn away from any personal sin that has given ground to my enemies, in Jesus' name.
11. I cancel binding effect of evil put upon me from any source, in Jesus' name.
12. I destroy enemy rights to afflict my plans to get married in Jesus' name.
13. I command stones that are blocking my marital breakthrough to be rolled away in Jesus' name.
14. I claim my right match, in Jesus' name.

Open doors and Profitable Employment

The Lord will make you the head, not the tail. If you pay attention to the commands of the Lord your God that I give you this day and carefully follow them, you will always be at the top, never at the bottom (Deuteronomy 28:13).

In the Lord's hand the king's heart is a stream of water that he channels toward all who please him (Proverbs 21:1).

Shout and be glad, Daughter Zion. For I am coming, and I will live among you," declares the Lord (Zechariah 2:10).

You have made them a little lower than the angels and crowned them with glory and honor (Psalms 8:5).

And to know this love that surpasses knowledge—that you may be filled to the measure of all the fullness of God. Now to him who is able to do immeasurably more than all we ask or imagine, according to his power that is at work within us (Ephesians 3:19-20).

For his anger lasts only a moment, but his favor lasts a lifetime weeping may stay for the night, but rejoicing comes in the morning (Psalms 30:5).

Now God had caused the official to show favour and compassion to Daniel (Daniel 1:9).

From now on, let no one cause me trouble, for I bear on my body the marks of Jesus (Galatians 6:17).

I can do all this through him who gives me strength. And my God will meet all your needs according to the riches of his glory in Christ Jesus (Philippians 4:13, 19).

1. Thank God, for only Him can advance you.
2. Father God, bring me into favour with those who will decide on my employment, in Jesus' name.
3. Father God, cause a divine substitution to happen so I can move ahead, in Jesus' name.
4. Father God, remove or change all humans agents stopping my employment, in Jesus' name.
5. Father God, catapult me into greatness as you did for Daniel in land of Babylon, in Jesus' name.
6. I bind every strong man delegated to hinder my progress today, in Jesus' name.

I will like to hear and read your testimonies. Share them:

All Nations Christian Centre
15 York Hill, West Norwood, London
SE27 0BU
Tel (+44) 20 8670 0300
admin@anccministries.org
www.anccministries.org

You are welcome to join us whenever you want to.

Sunday Celebration service: 10am
Wednesday: 7pm

Stay blessed and live free!

www.ingramcontent.com/pod-product-compliance
Lightning Source LLC
Chambersburg PA
CBHW070945080526
44587CB00015B/2229